MOLDERS OF
THE MEDIEVAL MIND

*The Influence of the Fathers
of the Church
on the Medieval Schoolmen*

BY

REV. FRANK P. CASSIDY, PH.D.

MOLDERS OF
THE MEDIEVAL MIND

*The Influence of the Fathers
of the Church
on the Medieval Schoolmen*

BY

REV. FRANK P. CASSIDY, PH.D.

KENNIKAT PRESS, INC./PORT WASHINGTON, N. Y.

NIHIL OBSTAT

Edward B. Jordan, A.M., S.T.D.

Censor Deputatus

IMPRIMATUR

✠ Michael J. Curley

Archiepiscopus
Baltimorensis-
Washingtonensis

MOLDERS OF THE MEDIEVAL MIND

Copyright 1944 by B. Herder Book Co.
Reissued in 1966 by Kennikat Press by arrangement

Library of Congress Catalog Card No: 66-25903

Manufactured in the United States of America

Analysed in the ESSAY & GENERAL LITERATURE INDEX

INTRODUCTION

THE present study is concerned with the influence of the Fathers of the Church on the Schoolmen of the Middle Ages. The leading educational movement of the Middle Ages was Scholasticism. It was a movement of immense proportions extending over that wide range of time from Boethius in the sixth century to Erasmus in the sixteenth. The immediate predecessors of the Scholastics were the Fathers of the Church. It was they who gave inspiration and direction to the achievements of the scholastic system of education, and impressed the Schoolmen with the importance of philosophy and theology so that the science of God became the monument of medieval learning.

The object, then, of this study is to point out the significance of the Church Fathers and their educational principles as molders of the medieval mind. Only those details of their lives have been given which seemed to be necessary for a comprehensive view of their environment and the opposing forces which they had to contend with; at the same time it is felt that these details will serve to show them in

[iii]

correct perspective in their relation to one another.

The section dealing with St. John Chrysostom was published in the March, 1942, issue of the *Catholic Education Review*. The account of the educational accomplishments of the Church Fathers is prefaced by a condensed treatment of Roman schools and education because of the influence of the seven liberal arts on their intellectual formation. There is also a chapter dealing with early Christian education in which the eternal pedagogical principles of Christ as the great teacher and educator of mankind are briefly outlined.

The literature dealing with the patristic period is so vast that the writer makes no claim to acquaintance with more than a minor part of it. The student will find satisfactory bibliographies in Bardenhewer's *Patrologie* and *Geschichte der altkirchlichen Litteratur* in five volumes; and also in De Labriolle's *Histoire de la littérature latine chrétienne*. The footnotes in the latter, together with the tables grouped at the end of the volume, are rich in bibliographical material. For the use of the general reader a selected bibliography of books accessible in English is given in the present work.

In the preparation of the following pages the author has had a deep sympathy with St. Jerome, who complained that his predecessors had already said so much better what he wished to say. That the reader may not have to search far to find something

[iv]

worth-while in this book is the ardent wish of the writer.

It is his agreeable duty to acknowledge his debt to the following kind colleagues: Dr. Martin R. P. McGuire, Dean of the Graduate School of Arts and Sciences of The Catholic University of America, Rt. Rev. Monsignor Edward B. Jordan, S.T.D., Vice-Rector of the University and former head of the Department of Education of the University, and Rev. Dr. John K. Cartwright of the University staff, who read the manuscript and made valuable suggestions concerning it.

He gladly makes acknowledgment of his indebtedness to publishers who have graciously permitted the use of quotations. Special acknowledgment is made to Burns, Oates and Washbourne, London; The Christian Literature Company, New York; T & T Clark, Ltd., London; Harvard University Press, Cambridge, Massachusetts; Hatchette et Cie, Paris; William Heinemann, Ltd. (Loeb), London; Houghton Mifflin Company, New York; John Murray, London; Charles Scribner's Sons, New York.

Frank P. Cassidy

The Catholic University of America

CONTENTS

CONTENTS

MOLDERS OF
THE MEDIEVAL MIND

CHAPTER I

ROMAN SCHOOLS AND EDUCATION

▰▰▰▰▰▰▰▰▰▰▰▰▰▰▰▰▰▰▰▰▰▰▰▰▰▰▰▰▰▰▰▰

THE Fathers of the Church have exercised a powerful and lasting influence on Christian education. Since Christianity developed within the limits of the Roman Empire, an inquiry into the educational achievements of the Church Fathers makes necessary an introductory study of Roman schools and education. In Rome, from its world-wide dominion, ultimately converged the various streams of culture flowing from Greece, from Egypt, and from the Orient; and from Rome this intellectual treasure has been bequeathed to the Western world.

The Romans belonged to the same racial family as the Greeks, but Roman education presents a strong contrast to Greek education. The Greeks determined the ideals of culture, but the Romans elaborated the institutional organization necessary for realizing these ideals. The Greeks were imaginative and impulsive in action; the Romans were matter-of-fact and judged all things by their usefulness.

[1]

Passing from Athens to Rome is as passing from poetry to prose; from an artist's picnic to a business house.[1]

The Romans specialized in social organization and law. The ideals of modern life have been derived largely from Greek and Hebrew sources, but the institutions of modern life originated largely with the Romans. The Roman genius for organization showed itself particularly in its military and political institutions, the effectiveness of which is seen in the great world empire that Rome achieved. This empire embraced southern and western Europe, western Asia, and the northern portion of Africa, and included the most diverse peoples and races. Its citizens paid taxes into the same treasury, were tried by the same law, and looked to the same armies for protection. The body of civil law organized by the Romans is even today the basis of the legal systems of most of the Western world.

From the standpoint of educational development, the history of the Roman nation may be divided into three periods: the purely Roman period, from the founding of the city to 250 B.C., when education was domestic and civic in nature and characteristically practical; the transitional period, extending from 250 B.C. to the conquest of Greece by the Romans in 146 B.C., when domestic education largely prevailed, but through contact with the

[1] Davidson, *A History of Education*, p 106.

[2]

Hellenic world Greek educational ideals were absorbed by Rome; and the Graeco-Roman period, from 146 B.C., to the fall of the Empire in A.D. 476, when the culture of the nation was actually Hellenized.

EARLY ROMAN EDUCATION

During the old Roman period there were apparently few schools and these were conducted by slaves and freedmen. The Roman family was the school for true Romans. Father and mother trained their children to habits of virtue essential for the exercise of individual rights and the discharge of personal duties and obligations. They regarded the religion of the Roman state as the religion of the family enlarged. Reading and writing were from early times accomplishments acquired by the child from his parents. From the fourth century these elementary arts for purposes of utility were probably as widely known among certain classes of Roman citizens as they were in civilized Europe at the beginning of the eighteenth century.[2] Arithmetic, too, was commonly studied by the child. The three R's may be said to be the ordinary maximum for the vast majority of the Roman people. The education was essentially not instruction but training. The boy

[2] Laurie, *Historical Survey of Pre-Christian Education*, p. 323.

learned by imitating his father, and the girl by imitating her mother.

The only literary training seems to have been based on the Laws of the Twelve Tables. These laws, engraved on twelve tablets, defined crimes and penalties and dealt with various matters of property rights, personal rights, and legal procedures. In fact, the laws formed a large part of the content of education in the early period. They were memorized along with national ballads and religious songs.

The boy's physical education was largely in the form of exercise gotten from the daily routine of farm work. It is true that in the home the child romped and played; and various games of ball were encouraged among younger boys and girls. Most of the Roman fathers were farmers, but they were ready to turn from the plow to the sword; consequently they trained their sons from boyhood to the use of arms. The physical education of the girl, which was under the direction of her mother, was gotten from the training she received in the performance of her household duties and in the arts of spinning and weaving wool.

At the age generally of sixteen the boy took off the *toga praetexta* and, putting on the *toga virilis*, entered upon the duties of a citizen. From now on he was for the most part in the company of his father. Specific military exercises were given him in the military camps. If he was a patrician, he learned

[4]

the responsibilities of citizenship by listening to discussions of practical matters of state business. If he was a plebeian, he worked with his father on the farm or in the shop.

THE PERIOD OF TRANSITION

When Rome began to extend her political and military power outside the Italian peninsula, her people came in contact with other civilizations, notably the Greek. Consequently the Greek language became more current in Rome, and the patricians often had their children instructed in it. Education, however, as in previous centuries, was mainly domestic. Although an occasional school is referred to, education in the true sense was not in the hands of school teachers. Cultured Greeks who were brought to Rome as slaves, upon obtaining their freedom, opened schools in which they would teach Greek to Roman youths. One of these, Livius Andronicus, undertook to supply the want of a literature by translating the *Odyssey* into Latin about 233 B.C. This translation served to train the young Roman to a better knowledge of his mother tongue and prepared the way for the first beginnings of Latin literature.

The elementary schools set up by these teachers were known as *ludi* (from *ludus*, meaning sport or play). Why *ludus* was the regular term for the elementary school cannot be answered satisfactorily.[3] It may have been so called because it was intended to supplement the more informal training of the home.[4] It may very well be that the designation was carefully made, lest some other name might act as a deterrent and discourage attendance.[5] The curriculum of the school included reading, writing, and counting. These subjects were taught through the medium of historical anecdotes, ballads, religious songs, and the Twelve Tables. By the beginning of the first century B.C., the Twelve Tables had been displaced by the Latinized *Odyssey* of Andronicus.

The conservative Romans were opposed to the rising Greek influence. Roman youths journeyed to Greek centers of learning to study rhetoric and philosophy, and Greek philosophers and rhetoricians appeared in Rome. At first a fad, it was now a common practice of the rich to have a Greek slave as tutor for their children. Schools began to multiply though they were looked upon with suspicion, partly because the Greek teachers were held in disfavor and partly because they charged fees, a procedure contrary to custom even in the Roman law courts.[6] The leader of the opposition was Cato the Elder (234–148 B.C.), who considered the Greek in-

[3] H. Leclerq, "Ecole," *Dictionnaire d'archéologie chrétienne et de liturgie*, 4, 2, 1731.
[4] Monroe, *Text-Book in the History of Education*, p. 193.
[5] Wilkins, *Roman Education*, p. 43.
[6] Kane, *An Essay toward a History of Education*, p. 65.

fluence pernicious and branded the Greeks as "a good-for-nothing and unimprovable race." He claimed that a dissemination of Greek literature among the Romans would ruin the traditional fabric of Roman society. Through Cato's efforts, the senate in 161 B.C. ordered the expulsion of all philosophers and rhetoricians from Rome. Before Cato died, however, he realized that Greek influence had come into Rome to stay and in the end he himself studied Greek.[7]

No work of a pedagogical character from this period has been preserved. Cato's work *De liberis educandis*, written as a protest against the Hellenic idea of culture, especially in regard to the subjects of music and literature, was intended to show what the requisites were for the young Roman who wished to become an orator, physician, husbandman, warrior, or jurist.[8] Knowledge for its own sake was condemned. An orator must be a man of sound understanding and uprightness. Only a noble man can be a good orator. Cato's counsel for the improvement of young men in oratory has been preserved, "*Rem tene, verba sequentur*," that is, get a good grasp of your matter, and the words will follow. A collection of Cato's sayings was long current in the literature in use in Roman schools, and of these many

[7] Gwynn, *Roman Education from Cicero to Quintilian,* p. 56.
[8] Laurie, *op. cit.*, p. 328.

[7]

have been preserved in Plutarch. A list of precepts bearing his name was also studied in the schools of the Middle Ages.

Two years after the death of Cato, 146 B.C., Greece became a Roman possession. Greek art treasures, Greek scholars, and even complete libraries were transferred to Rome by the conquerors. Along with this culture came the educational ideas basic to it. From this period onward the triumph of Greek influence upon Roman education is apparent. Rome had conquered Greece, yet Greece in turn conquered Rome according to the oft-quoted words of Horace: *Graecia capta ferum victorem cepit.* The Romans appropriated Greek literature, but they did not cultivate literature for its own sake. The Greek language was an essential element in a liberal Roman education, but the aim of the literary education was oratory. This fusion of Greek culture with Roman is best seen in the system of schools which the Romans developed in the Graeco-Roman period.

GRAECO-ROMAN PERIOD

This amalgamation of Roman education with the Greek was well established by the first century B.C. and remained unmodified until the latter part of the second century of our era, when the spirit of Roman culture declined. Out of this new type of education developed three levels of instruction: the elementary, the *ludus* or school of the *litterator;* the secondary, grammar schools taught by the *grammatici;* and the higher, the schools of rhetoric taught by the *rhetores*. Advanced courses of study were obtainable in higher schools of learning.

About the *ludus* little is accurately known. The entrance age was probably six or seven. Reading, writing, and the simple operations of arithmetic were learned. The reading book was the *Odyssey* in Latin. The methods of instruction were memoriter and imitative. The memory was cultivated by having the child learn by heart many maxims and practical selections. The alphabet and all kinds of combinations of syllables were taught before words were learned. The pupil wrote on wax tablets with the stylus; and the teacher guided his hand in his first efforts to trace the letters. The fingers and pebbles were used to learn how to count; further steps in numeration were taught by means of the abacus; and sums were worked upon the tablets. The discipline of the school was severe, and the rod was in frequent use. A favorite form of punishment was to have a boy held on the shoulders of another while the master beat him upon the bare back.[9] It was customary to have the *pedagogus* accompany the boy to and from school. Very often he taught the boy, usually conversational Greek.

[9] Graves, *History of Education*, I, 247 ff.

As there were no set fees and no school houses in our sense of the term, the *litterator* had to take what he could get and provide his own schoolroom. Any serviceable place was looked upon as good enough for elementary instruction. School was held in the open air, in some quiet corner of a street or market place. Instruction was also given on a veranda or in a lean-to attached to a shop or to a house. The *litterator* was in business the same as any other shop-keeper; his shop was a place where an elementary education could be gotten.[10] No real qualifications were required of him, and naturally his position in society was very humble.

The *grammaticus* was more esteemed, yet up to imperial times his social standing was low. The instruction given by him was more advanced than that of the *litterator*, but in part it was the same. The increasing literary work of the *ludus* gave rise to the grammar schools. These furnished the secondary education upon which the pupil entered about the age of twelve. The Greek grammar school was the first in origin and was usually attended first. With the rise of Latin literature in the first century before Christ, the Latin grammar school came into favor. Grammar was the chief study, but grammar had a wider meaning for the Roman than it has now; it included the study of literature as well as language. Special attention was paid to the style of the

10 Leclerq, *op. cit.*, pp. 1732 f.

authors used as models for writing and speaking. Homer was the first of the Greek poets studied, and others, like the didactic poet Hesiod and the dramatists, Aeschylus, Sophocles, and Euripides, were introduced. In the Latin schools, Vergil and later Horace, Lucan, and Statius were studied.

Great importance was attached to purity of diction and good expression. For this reason the best authors were paraphrased, and exercises in diction and verse writing were common. Drill was given in the parts of speech and syntax. Dictation was largely practiced with a view to correct spelling. By means of dictation, select poems could be written down and learned by heart when the complete works of the poet could not be had. Even when rolls became cheap, the practice of dictation was continued.[11]

In the course of time the quadrivium or mathematical subjects—arithmetic, music, geometry, astronomy—were taught, evidently gotten from the Hellenic learning. Geography, history, natural sciences, and mythology were touched upon because of their connection with the literature. Gymnastics was also a part of the course. All the subjects were pursued with the same practical purpose that everywhere differentiates Roman education from Greek. Arithmetic was mere calculation; geometry was closely related to mensuration; astronomy served to

[11] Laurie, *op. cit.*, p. 338.

determine the calendar; music aided in the appreciation of poetry and the acquisition of oratorical power; gymnastic exercises were mostly for military training.[12]

The accommodations for these secondary schools were far superior to those of the elementary schools. They were provided with benches for the pupils and a high seat for the master. The assistant sat on a stool. The benches had no backs. The pupils wrote with pen and ink on parchment placed on their knees. The schoolrooms were sometimes adorned with mural art pieces.[13]

The secondary education of the Roman youth was usually completed when he assumed the toga. His further education depended on his vocation in life. The farmer engaged in farming; the soldier passed into the service of the army; and the lawyer or statesman entered upon his professional training in the rhetorical school.

The rhetorical school, which provided a course of two or three years, developed out of the practice of debate which had gradually grown up in the grammar school. It was a professional school offering a legal and forensic training. The rhetorical school was concerned immediately with the technique of oratory so that it gave a practical training in declamation with special attention to intonation,

[12] McCormick, *History of Education*, p. 57.
[13] Laurie, *op. cit.*, p. 346.

articulation, and other elements of delivery. Eulogies and pleas for plaintiffs and defendants were delivered by the student and criticized by the master. It was generally agreed, however, that the orator should have a knowledge of many fields of learning as a cultural background. For this reason the rhetorical school undertook to give the student a good training in literature from the point of view of composition and style, and instructed him in the quadrivium as well as in history, law, and philosophy. The rhetorical schools of imperial times often provided advanced instruction in the seven liberal arts.

The seven liberal arts were the constituents of general culture. Long before the fall of the Roman Empire differentiation of learning into subjects occurred. Cato, in order to oppose Greek education and manners, drew up a curriculum characteristically Roman. It included oratory, agriculture, law, war, medicine. Half a century later, when Greek influence had largely prevailed, Varro wrote upon most of the subjects in the Greek curriculum: grammar, rhetoric, dialectic, arithmetic, geometry, astronomy, music, and philosophy, besides many others.[14] The liberal arts were held by the ancients

[14] At the opening of the Christian era no definite number had been fixed for the liberal arts, either at Athens, Alexandria, or Rome. Quintilian, in his treatise on education which had an abiding influence on the pedagogy of succeeding ages, divided all education into grammar and rhetoric; he advocated

to be preparatory to the study of philosophy. The Fathers of the Church accepted this point of view, but went a step further by declaring that philosophy and all its preparatory studies were preparation for an understanding of Christian theology.

After completing his course in the rhetorical school, the ambitious young Roman might go to the great university schools for a higher training. In addition to Athens other distinguished philosophical and rhetorical centers were to be found at Rhodes, Apollonia, Mitylene, Alexandria, Tarsus, Pergamus, Constantinople, Marseilles, Smyrna, and Ephesus. In such centers libraries had been established, and distinguished rhetoricians were to be found.

----

that the orator study a little music, geometry, and astronomy. St. Augustine wrote a treatise on grammar and music and stated that he intended to write on five other liberal studies. Judging from the work of Martianus Capella, the branches taught in the better schools of the Roman Empire in the fourth and fifth centuries were grammar, dialectic, rhetoric, geometry, arithmetic, astronomy, and music. In his treatise, Capella lays no stress upon their number. The first actual use of the numeral seven in connection with the liberal arts is said to occur in the *De clericorum institutione* of Rabanus Maurus in the ninth century. Cf. Thomas Davidson, "The Seven Liberal Arts," *Educational Review*, II, 467–72. Abelson claims that the first use of the phrase "the seven liberal arts" in Christian literature is found in Cassiodorus' *De Artibus et Disciplinis Liberalium Literarum* in which he gives scriptural sanction for these studies by the analogy of the seven pillars of wisdom. Cf. Paul Abelson, *The Seven Liberal Arts* (New York: Teachers College, 1906), p. 9.

A discussion of the aims and methods of the best type of Graeco-Roman school, whether grammatical or rhetorical, is to be found in Quintilian's educational treatise *De institutione oratoria*. Important elements of the Roman theory of education are also revealed in Cicero's *De oratore;* in Suetonius' *De grammaticis* and *De rhetoricis;* and in the *De oratoribus* of Tacitus. As the orator is the highest type of the educated Roman, all set up the orator as the ideally educated man. All maintain that the orator should have a knowledge of practically the entire realm of knowledge and that he should be primarily a good man.

Under the prevailing educational system were produced the great Latin authors of the Golden Age—the prose writers: Cicero, Caesar, Sallust, Livy; and the poets: Lucretius, Catullus, Vergil, Horace, and Ovid. In comparison, the succeeding age is called the Silver Age, although it yielded great classic names like Seneca, the philosopher; Quintilian, the educator; Tacitus, the historian; Juvenal, the satirist; and Pliny, the letter writer.[15] Although the debt of these worthies to the varied literature of Greece is obvious, as Romans they borrowed in a Roman way and made their borrowings their own and their country's. It is true that their literary compositions were unknown to the masses of the people because their Latin was not

[15] Duff, *The Writers of Rome*, p. 29.

everyday speech; still it was different only in degree. It was more refined and accurate in grammar and diction, but it was the same Latin.[16]

In the second century of the Christian era began a long succession of Christian apologists who profited by Cicero's development of a philosophical diction. In the language of Rome they defended the faith and originated a wealth of patristic literature. This spiritual invasion of the stronghold of pagan culture by Tertullian, Minucius Felix, Cyprian, Arnobius, and Lactantius forms a kind of late parallel to the bygone invasion of Rome by Hellenism. Although this Christian influence was later in some aspects anti-literary because Augustine lamented the time that he wasted in shedding tears over the distress of Queen Dido in Vergil, the Latin scholarship of Jerome on the other hand found expression in the Vulgate, which exerted a powerful influence on medieval and Church Latin.[17]

After the second century with the decadence of Roman society, education was a distinction of the aristocracy. Training in oratory became formal and artificial because education had no practical purpose; yet it was a necessary qualification for entering the senatorial class. Schools, however, were to be found everywhere. They were subsidized by the emperors; the grammarians and rhetoricians were

[16] *Ibid.*, p. 9.
[17] *Ibid.*, p. 13.

esteemed and rewarded. With few exceptions teachers contented themselves with formal speech. Wandering lecturers went from one city to another displaying the artificialities of their superficial thinking. They were, like the early sophists of Greece, concerned not with the truth of what they said but with facility of expression in saying it.

The Roman system of education had become a hollow formality, a mere shell. The masses of Italy were not interested in schools; they were idle and poor. But conditions in the provinces were better. Grammatical and rhetorical schools flourished especially in Gaul, Spain, and Africa. These schools continued to give a formal training in pagan learning down to the close of the sixth century. Meanwhile ancient culture had degenerated; Christian culture was in the ascendancy. The new educators were the Fathers of the Church.

CHAPTER II

CHRISTIANITY AND EARLY WESTERN CIVILIZATION

▪▪

WHEN the Fathers of the Church come on the scene, Christianity with its universal gospel is about to become a world dominating faith. At the close of the first century Christians were to be found in every country bordering on the Mediterranean.

RAPID PROPAGATION OF THE NEW FAITH

The causes that contributed to the rapid propagation of Christianity were many. The teachings of the eminent pagan philosophers—Socrates, Plato, Aristotle, and Zeno—had exercised an ennobling influence upon the minds of the educated class and prepared the way for the acceptance of Christian morality. Many pagans through contact with Jews had embraced the worship of the true God and looked forward to the coming of the Messiah. Converts to the new faith were to be found among the rich and the poor, the noble and the lowly. Men and women from every class of society were represented—officials of Caesar's household; the proconsul of Cyprus, Sergius Paulus; the noble women of Beroea; the principal women of Thessalonica; the physician Luke, the scholar Apollo; Dionysius, a judge of the Athenian Areopagus, as well as countless others who became Christians in the Jewish communities stretching from the Tigris to the Tagus.[1]

The widespread dissemination of the new religion was owing in part to the facilities for travel provided by an extensive network of communication; a splendid system of highways connected the capital of the Roman Empire with every province and its important cities. Zealous missioners were soon joined to the apostles; and within an incredibly brief time Christianity was preached throughout the vast empire of Rome. The new faith was taught on the fertile plains of the Mesopotamian valley and the tablelands of Syria and Asia Minor. Christian doctrine was known in the Delta of the Nile and along the great river in Ethiopia, in the African oasis of Cyrene, and in the island of Cyprus, in Spain and Gaul.[2]

Moreover, a knowledge of Greek as the vehicle of polite intercourse and of Latin as the language of

[1] Shahan, *The Beginnings of Christianity*, p. 24.
[2] *Ibid.*, pp. 23 f.

the Roman in everyday life was sufficient for the evangelization of the East and West; while the Roman genius for organization developed a respect for law and social order that prepared the Graeco-Roman world for the development of the Christian standard which properly determined the relationships of the individual to society.

Another cause contributing to the remarkable growth of the early Church was the number of miracles wrought by God in her ministrations, particularly during the first three centuries. Origen declares that he personally had seen many miracles performed. The heroic fortitude with which the Christian martyrs faced death rather than give up the faith inspired others to become converts so that their blood, as Tertullian says, became the seed of Christianity. The apostolic zeal of converted philosophers and rhetoricians, such as Justin Martyr, Clement of Alexandria, and Lactantius, for the conversion of their former associates is evidence of the incomparable enthusiasm displayed in the work of promoting the holy cause. But the real source of the vitality of Christian truth and its unmistakable mission in the life and character of mankind is to be found in its divine Founder, the God-man and Redeemer, Jesus Christ.

New Conception of Life

With the Christian idea of life came new ideals in culture and education which revolutionized the whole development of Western civilization. Christianity taught that in Jesus a new principle of divine life had entered the human race and the natural world, a principle by which mankind is raised to a higher order. God had arranged everything from the beginning with a view to the perfection of man. The purpose of creation finds its complete fulfillment in the incarnate Word. The world process is regarded not as a static order governed by the fatal law of necessity, but as a divine drama unfolding the story of the creation and fall of man, his redemption, and his glorious restoration.[3]

St. Gregory of Nyssa sees in the Incarnation the source of a new movement of regeneration which leads ultimately to the deification of human nature by its participation in the divine life. With the other Church Fathers in the East he labored to put in a form accessible to the Greek mind the Christian doctrine of man and the Incarnation in an attempt to express the new Christian world view. Their efforts resulted in Byzantine religion tending to become absorbed in theological speculation re-

[3] Dawson, *Progress and Religion*, p. 156.

garding the nature of the Godhead, a tendency which reached its climax in the writings of Dionysius, the Pseudo-Areopagite.

In the Roman West, Christianity became a dynamic moral and social force. Long before the fall of the Empire the Western Church had to contend with the forces of barbarism and social disorder. It did not become incorporated in a fixed social or political system as the Byzantine Church did. Western Catholicism was concerned not with speculative theology but with matters of Church order, with the problems of moral conduct and moral responsibility. This emphasis on the social aspect of Christian culture led the Church Fathers in the West to assume an important attitude toward the state. Hilary of Poitiers vehemently attacked the interference of the state in religious matters. St. Ambrose is the champion of the authority of the spiritual power, declaring that it is the duty of the Christian ruler to subordinate his action to the Church's authority in all matters that concern the faith. The ideal of St. Augustine is the City of God in which the spiritual order is revealed, not as a static metaphysical principle, but as a dynamic force manifesting itself in human society.[4]

[4] Dawson, *op. cit.*, pp. 158–64.

New Social Gospel

The Incarnation did not destroy or supersede nature. It did not replace old ideals; it included them. The institution of Christianity set all the things of time against a background of eternity. Paganism looked upon man as a being created only for a temporal destiny, and his education was determined largely according to that point of view.

Christianity supplied the true determinants which were lacking in pagan education, to make known man's true destiny, to render a true appreciation of his worth. The Christian has a new dignity; he has been made a son of God by adoption and an heir to the heavenly kingdom. For that reason his education is much more comprehensive than that of a pagan. He must combine the supernatural aids given him by Jesus Christ with current needs of life.[5] His sojourn on earth is but a preparation for the real life to come. His task is an endless struggle to be in the world, yet not of it.[6] He must strive for the harmonious use of body and soul in this life, yet direct all his efforts to a goal beyond that of the present. He must labor with the conviction that he has not here a lasting city, but seeks one that is to come.[7]

The true ideal of Christianity was expressed in its

[5] Kane, *An Essay Toward a History of Education*, pp. 75 f.
[6] John 17:15.
[7] Heb. 13:14.

[23]

new social gospel of charity and love. Pagan imperialism did not realize the nobility and dignity of mankind and did not treat men as brothers. Subjection of men, women, and children to the whims and purposes of those who held power was the ruling principle of pagan social life. Christ taught that God is no respecter of persons, that there are no castes or classes among men, that the spirit of charity must be the very palladium of national power, the very dynamic of civilization—real human brotherhood under the fatherhood of God. "This is My commandment, that you love one another as I have loved you." [8]

There was no question of bondsman or free; all men were equal in the sight of God. Woman was declared to be, not the slave of man, but his companion; she was restored to her rightful position in the home and in society. Marriage was raised to the dignity of a sacrament; and children were held to be God's most precious gifts. The doctrine of the brotherhood of man struck at all racial hatreds and the traditional conceptions of patriotism; condemned pagan inequality in economic life within nations and between nations; and denounced selfish gain and personal aggrandizement. The kingdom of God was not of this world, but a kingdom in the hearts of men. His kingdom must prevail if a new social order were to reign in the world.

[8] John 15:12.

The Perfect Teacher

These glorious principles justly entitle Jesus
Christ to be called the great Teacher and Educator of mankind. The truths taught by Him have
had a profound influence in shaping educational
theory and practice for two thousand years; and
they are the inspiration of what is best in modern
educational thought. Christ is the perfect Teacher.
In His infinite wisdom, He possessed all the qualifications of the divine Master, having a complete
knowledge of the nature and the purpose of each
created thing. His method of teaching must have
reflected this perfection. Consequently He is the
model of teaching effectiveness in educational meth-
odology.

In His personality, Christ is the ideal Teacher.
His life and His teachings have been subjected to a
most careful examination by rationalists and skep-
tics, but critical research reveals that His personality challenges analysis. The ideal qualities which are
found in Him are bewildering because they seem to
be the very antithesis of one another.

In His character, authority is allied with humility,
justice with forbearance, wisdom with simplicity,
austerity with sympathy; yet these qualities are
blended into such a complete harmony that He is
recognized by the great and the small as the ideal

Person.[9] His voice was magnetic; His presence inspiring. His apostles bowed in admiration before the sublime teachings of the Son of man. They called Him Rabbi—Master. The people in general were eager to hear Him, so attractive were His manner and doctrine. They proclaimed Him a great teacher, one speaking with power and authority.[10]

Christ had but one aim: to bring men to God by revealing to them a new goal and purpose for their striving. He commanded His disciples, "Seek ye therefore first the kingdom of God and His justice: and all these things shall be added unto you." [11] This is the cardinal principle which should govern the relative position of the lower and higher aims of life; while complementary to it is the principle of the Cross. "If any man will follow Me, let him deny himself and take up his cross and follow Me. For whosoever will save his life shall lose it: and whosoever shall lose his life for My sake and the gospel shall save it." [12] By revealing the immortality of goodness Christ held out to men the hope of a happy existence in a future and eternal life; man learned to seek the things that are above and not to be satisfied with the things that are upon the earth.

Our Lord's teaching procedure contains elements that show a complete mastery of the laws of learn-

[9] Marique, *History of Christian Education*, I, 27.
[10] Matt. 7:29.
[11] *Ibid.*, 6:33.
[12] Mark 8:34 f.

ing and exemplify the eternal principles of pedagogy. He applied the principle of apperception which is basic to teaching efficiency. A large part of teaching is perception building. The new material a teacher gives the pupil must be referred to previously acquired backgrounds for recognition and understanding. Whatever is learned that is new must be learned in terms of what is already known. The methods of instruction used by Christ were admirably adapted to the previous knowledge and experience of His hearers. Whatever His audience, He used language that was intelligible to all; when speaking to the multitudes, He used a plain style; when addressing the leaders of the people, He used a manner of speech suitable to an educated class. His discourses abound in parables which make reference to familiar experiences of farmers, shepherds, fishermen, and the people generally. His concrete illustrations and examples drawn from simple phases of nature—the mustard seed, the tree and its fruit, the lilies of the field, the birds of the air, the sheepfold, the draught of fishes—correlated His sublime doctrine with the previous knowledge of His audience and provided for its retention.

Most noteworthy is the care that Christ took to prepare the minds of His hearers for the great truths of His message; the more difficult a truth was to understand, the more detailed was the preparation for the profound doctrine. The teaching of the

Real Presence had been foreshadowed by the miracle of the multiplication of the loaves and fishes and, according to the sixth chapter of St. John, the doctrine was not given until the multitude was ready to grasp its meaning. Christ repeatedly referred to the various books of the Old Testament, to the names and sayings of the patriarchs, the kings and the prophets, with which the people were familiar, as prefiguring the fullness of truth in the Christian dispensation.[13]

The principle of self-activity found expression in Christ's teaching. He wished His followers to be "doers of the word and not hearers only." He urged them to translate belief into action. "Not everyone that saith to Me, Lord, Lord, shall enter the kingdom of heaven: but he that doth the will of My Father." [14] His doctrine appealed to the imagination of His hearers and stimulated thinking. He gently rebuked those who entertained questions but hesitated to ask them.

The principle of individual differences was respected by Christ. He recognized the needs and capacities of the individual whom He instructed. When He conversed with the learned Nicodemus His approach to the truth was quite different from His method when He talked with the unlettered Samaritan woman. With the former, He entered

[13] McCormick, *History of Education,* pp. 67 f.
[14] Matt. 7:21.

into a discussion of the most profound doctrines, saying: "Art thou a master in Israel, and knowest not these things?" [15] With the latter, He pointed to the well and said: "Whosoever drinketh of this water shall thirst again. . . . But the water that I will give him shall become in him a fountain of water." [16]

The doctrine of imitation and the principle of motivation are also exemplified in Christ's method of teaching. He utilized the imitative impulse as a means of uplift and of salvation. "Be you therefore perfect, as also your heavenly Father is perfect." [17] "The disciple is not above his master; but every one shall be perfect if he be as his master." [18] He aroused an active interest in His doctrines through an appeal to the associated interests of His listeners. Love was the motive He constantly used to lift up the mind to a view of immaterial truths. "As the Father hath loved Me, I also have loved you." "If you keep My commandments, you shall abide in My love: as I also have kept My Father's commandments and do abide in His love." "Greater love than this no man hath, that a man lay down his life for his friends." [19]

No one was dearer to the heart of Christ than the

[15] John 3:10.
[16] John 4:13.
[17] Matt. 5:48.
[18] Luke 6:40.
[19] John 15:9 f., 13.

child. When the disciples rebuked those who had brought to Him young children, He was displeased and said to them: "Suffer the little children to come unto Me and forbid them not; for of such is the kingdom of God." [20] He loved little children and, setting a child in the midst of His disciples, He taught them, saying: "Whosoever therefore shall humble himself as this little child, he is the greater in the kingdom of heaven." [21] He cautions His disciples that the innocence and tender years of children must be carefully guarded. "But he that shall scandalize one of these little ones that believe in Me, it were better for him that a millstone should be hanged about his neck, and that he should be drowned in the depth of the sea." [22]

No less significant in the method of Christ's teaching is the fact that He taught with authority. "You call Me Master and Lord. And you say well: for so I am." [23] Without authority education is impossible. His noble life exemplified respect for law, obedience to authority. Authority of the natural law, of parent and teacher, authority of Church and state, are fundamental concepts of His educational principles. For the guidance of all teachers He laid down the immortal principle that the primary function of true teaching is to impart the truth. "And

[20] Mark 10:14.
[21] Matt. 18:4.
[22] Ibid., 18:6.
[23] John 13:13.

you shall know the truth: and the truth shall make you free." [24] Christ is the noble example of the teacher practicing the truth that He teaches. He was for the multitudes of His own time and He is for every one of us today the living model of the truths that He proclaimed. "And learn of Me, because I am meek, and humble of heart." [25]

These and similar educational principles bequeathed by Christ to the world are the substance of the *pedagogia perennis* of Catholicism; they have always animated the organic teaching of His Church. In accordance with His teachings these principles have been consistently expounded by the great leaders of Christian thought from the Apostolic Age and the era of the Church Fathers to the present day.

THE TEACHING CHURCH

Christ came to save all men. His doctrine was the living and everlasting truth. He declared that His gospel should be preached throughout the whole world and to all nations, and it was for this purpose that He made His Church a teaching body under the guidance of the Spirit of truth. The charter by which the Church has been constituted the greatest teaching agency of all times is found in the words

[24] *Ibid.*, 8:32.
[25] Matt. 11:29.

of Christ to His apostles: "Going therefore, teach ye all nations: baptizing them in the name of the Father and of the Son and of the Holy Ghost. Teaching them to observe all things whatsoever I have commanded you. And behold I am with you all days, even to the consummation of the world." [26]

Through the exercise of this divine commission, the Church became the prolific mother of schools and established the great ideals of Christian life. The history of Christian education amply shows that the Church has an abiding interest in every wholesome human activity. As age has succeeded age, it is the Church that has been the greatest patron of science and art, and it is in her that architecture, sculpture, painting, and learning have found their best support. Scholarly historians and sociologists recognize the wonderful educational work accomplished by the Catholic Church.

During the first two centuries Christian education was almost exclusively moral and religious. The main concern of the Church was the conversion of Jews and of pagans to Christianity. Her sacramental system was the divinely appointed educational means by which her children received supernatural assistance for living virtuous lives and for the development in their souls of a Christian character. Cyprian testifies that infant baptism was not uncommon from the early days of Christian-

[26] Matt. 28:19 f.

ity; [27] but the early Christians were mostly adults
who had some kind of training and education. They
had to be taught the Christian way of life and
needed religious instruction in the teachings of
Jesus Christ. During the centuries of persecution it
was customary to defer the baptism even of children of Christians to a mature age, the age of thirty
being regarded as the most appropriate. For that
reason religious instruction continued for years before the sacrament of baptism was conferred. But
as the Christians grew strong in numbers, and as
persecution diminished, the spiritual leaders in the
Church sought to educate the head as well as the
heart. They established schools in which the intellectual element was combined with the moral and
religious. They themselves became teachers and lent
every effort to further the doctrines of Christianity.
The first schools opened by the Church were the
catechumenal and catechetical schools.

CATECHUMENS

The catechumens were divided into two broad
groups, the simple catechumens and the *competentes*.[28] These catechumens included children of
believers, Jewish converts, and the adult converts
of the pagan population. They not only received an

[27] Cyprian, *Epist.* 59. Migne, *Patr. lat.*, III, 1015-18.
[28] F. X. Funk, "Die Katechumenklassen," *Theologische
Quartalschrift*, LXV (1883), 41.

intellectual formation, but also underwent a moral and liturgical discipline. Their instruction was intellectual as it had to do with doctrines, but it was to a large extent a moral discipline and a moral supervision. In the beginning the instructors in the catechumenal schools were the bishops, priests, and deacons; in later times other clerics and laymen held the office of catechist.

COMPETENTES

Before the aspirant for baptism was received into the school he was subjected to an examination of motives, which included an elementary instruction in the fundamental principles of revealed truth. If the examination was satisfactory, the aspirant was admitted into the group of *competentes*. His reception into the catechumenate was celebrated with certain rites in accordance with the custom of the locality. The signing with the cross, an insufflation, the imposition of hands, the tasting of salt, and an anointing with oil were among the ceremonies used in different dioceses.

The *competentes* were given a special place in church from which they listened to the lessons and homilies at Mass. Their presence explains the symbolic language prompted by the *disciplina arcani* [29]

[29] John H. Newman, *The Arians of the Fourth Century* (New York: Longmans, Green and Co., 1891), Part I, 41–79.

used in the patristic homilies. After the deacon asked the prayers of the congregation for them, and the bishop prayed over them, they were dismissed before the beginning of the Mass of the faithful. They were then instructed from the Scriptures in the portico in another special part of the church by a cleric or layman. The books of Wisdom, Ecclesiasticus, Tobias, Esther, and Judith were commonly chosen because of their moral content. The Gospels were used to acquaint them with the life of our Lord and the mission of the apostles.

Before Lent it was customary for the bishop to request those of the *competentes* who wished to receive baptism to give him their names. They were then examined to determine their fitness and, if found worthy, were regarded as *electi* or *illuminati* and now entered upon their second term of probation, which lasted throughout the forty days of Lent. This was a period of intensive doctrinal, liturgical, and ascetical preparation for baptism, during which the Creed and the Lord's Prayer were taught them orally with the understanding that they were to commit them to memory. Baptism was conferred on the vigil of Easter, followed immediately by confirmation. The newly baptized were given daily instructions during the ensuing week, and the festivities connected with the reception of these sacraments lasted over the whole of the Easter octave.

The catechumenate originated about the middle

of the second century, reached its height in the fourth and fifth, and gradually disappeared after the eighth. The length of the catechumenate depended upon the will of the bishop. In earlier times it was very short, but on account of the persecutions of the Christians, aspirants were declared competent to receive baptism only after years of probation. It became necessary to take precautions against the danger of apostasy or even betrayal. In later centuries the lengthening process served to prove that a complete moral conversion of the aspirant had taken place. The catechumens themselves often prolonged the period of probation, either because they feared the severity of Christian life or because they desired that their spiritual rebirth take place at the hour of death.[30]

Course of Instruction

The *Apostolic Constitutions* prescribed the following course of instruction for catechumens who sought admission into the Church:

Let him, therefore, who is to be taught the truth in regard to piety be instructed before his baptism in the knowledge of the unbegotten God, in the understanding of his only begotten Son, in the assured acknowledgement of the Holy Ghost. Let him learn the order of the several

[30] Fuerst, *The Systematic Teaching of Religion*, pp. 24–36.

parts of the creation, the series of providence, the different dispensations of the laws. Let him be instructed how the world was made, and why man was appointed to be a citizen therein; let him also know his own nature, of what sort it is; let him be taught how God punished the wicked with water and fire, and did glorify the saints in every generation—I mean Seth, and Enos, and Enoch, and Noah, and Abraham and his posterity, and Melchizedek, and Job, and Moses, and Joshua, and Caleb, and Phineas the priest, and those that were holy in every generation; and how God still took care of and did not reject mankind, but called them from their error and vanity to the acknowledgement of the truth at various seasons, reducing them from bondage and impiety unto liberty and piety, from injustice to righteousness, from death eternal to everlasting life. Let him that offers himself to baptism learn these and the like things during the time that he is a catechumen; and let him who lays his hands upon him adore God, the Lord of the whole world, and thank him for his creation, for his sending Christ his only begotten Son, that he might save man by blotting out his transgressions, and that he might remit ungodliness and sins, and might "purify him from all filthiness of flesh and spirit," and sanctify man according to the good pleasure of his kindness, that he might inspire him with the knowledge of his will, and enlighten the eyes of his heart to consider his wonderful works, and make known to him the judgments of righteousness, that so he might hate every way of iniquity, and walk in the way of truth, that he might be thought worthy of the laver of regeneration, to the adoption of sons, which is in Christ, that "being planted together in the likeness of the death of Christ," in hopes of a glorious communication, he may be mortified to sin, and may live to God; as to his mind, and word, and deed, and may be numbered together in the book of the living. And after this thanks-giving, let him instruct him in the doctrines concerning our Lord's incarnation, and in those concerning his passion and resurrection from the dead, and assumption.[31]

CATECHETICAL SCHOOLS

In the early centuries of Christianity the Christian faith was attacked by pagan adversaries, and the Fathers of the Church resorted to formal logic in order to counteract the metaphysical speculation of the four great sects—the Peripatetics, the Stoics, the Epicureans, and the Academicians. Greek philosophy had developed a profound interest in the systematic organization of thought. This interest was continued in the pagan and Jewish schools of the Graeco-Roman world. The systems of religious philosophy known collectively as "Hellenistic" were not in accord with the doctrines of Christianity and challenged the best efforts of the Fathers of the Church to keep clear and undistorted the vision of their educational ideal. To counteract the errors in the philosophic and religious speculations of the public schools in the leading centers of culture and to defend the deposit of faith, the Church gradually organized the catechetical school,[32] which was

[31] Cubberly, *Readings in the History of Education*, pp. 52 f.
[32] The catechumenal schools were also called catechetical schools from the use of the catechism as the basis of instruction

in reality the first Christian academy of philosophy and theology.

The earliest of these schools appeared about 160 at Rome under Justin Martyr. Other famous catechetical schools followed at Alexandria, Caesarea, Antioch, Edessa, Nisibis, Rhinocorura in Egypt, and Carthage. Tradition claims that the Alexandrian school was founded by St. Mark the Evangelist when he introduced Christianity into Egypt,[33] but that tradition is disputed. In Jerome's time it was commonly taught that St. Mark the Evangelist, upon the dispersion of the apostles, was sent by St. Peter to preach in Egypt. It is certain that Pantaenus gave catechetical instruction in the school at Alexandria in the year 179. The school at Caesarea under Origen soon rivaled that of Alexandria and, although at his death the institution declined, the reputation for learning which it had enjoyed was revived by Pamphilus, a former student of the Alexandrian school. The Christian school at Antioch was established by Melchion, a teacher of rhetoric. His successor Lucian, who had studied at Edessa, made Antioch famous for biblical exegesis and Christian theology. During the second half of the fourth century the

---

in subject-matter. The term catechetical is better applied to a development of the catechumenal school in certain localities into an institution of higher learning. Cf. Paul Monroe, *Text-Book in the History of Education* (New York: Macmillan Company, 1921), p. 233.

[33] Drane, *Christian Schools and Scholars*, p. 3.

management of the school at Antioch passed into the hands of St. John Chrysostom. Under his direction, it became a remarkable center of Christian culture and learning. St. Cyril, bishop of Jerusalem, was the distinguished head of the school in that city in the fourth century. He delivered there a series of catechetical lectures which are clear and logical explanations of the articles of faith.

About this same time the school at Edessa, which was established by the beginning of the third century, was considerably strengthened by St. Ephraem Syrus and a band of his disciples. He had been appointed headmaster of the school at Nisibis by his bishop, but when the city passed into the hands of the king of Persia he took up his abode in Roman territory at Edessa. He was the head of the school there until his death. In the second half of the fifth century Edessa became the seat of Nestorian Christianity and remained so for a period of fifty years, when the school was finally broken up by the Greek Emperor Zeno. The Nestorians then fled to Nisibis, where they established a new school.[34] It was through the agency of this school that the Christian Syrians initiated the Arabians into a knowledge of Greek science, medicine, mathematics, and the philosophy of Aristotle. The monk Dionysius was the catechist in the catechetical school at Rhinocorura

[34] Eby and Arrowood, *The History and Philosophy of Education Ancient and Medieval*, pp. 614 f.

in Egypt during the latter half of the fourth century. At the opening of the fifth century the catechetical school at Carthage, the primitive see of Northern Africa, merited distinction when, at the request of the deacon Deogratias, a successful catechist, St. Augustine wrote his treatise *De catechizandis rudibus*.

The greatest service of the catechetical schools was the production of theological literature, and the scholarly works they gave rise to may be ranked with the best produced by later universities in the field of theological and biblical research.[35] Moreover, these schools enrolled pagans as well as Christians, lay students as well as clerics, women as well as men, offering to them as good an education under Christian auspices as was given by the philosophers or teachers of pagan learning in the university centers of the Graeco-Roman world. There were no school buildings except the residence of the master. Here the pupils were received, and the master taught his classes or gave private instruction till late at night.[36] The course of study, like the curriculum of the Middle Ages, culminated in theology and, in

[35] Eby and Arrowood, *op. cit.*, p. 618.

[36] This type of school reached its greatest development in the eastern branch of the Roman Empire. There were approximately half a dozen good catechetical schools of the East and of Carthage in which really learned Christian scholars were produced; but the number of them, compared with the entire body of Christians, was decidedly small. Cf. W. Kane, *An Essay toward a History of Education*, p. 86.

the subjects taught preparatory to a full understanding of Christianity, the Fathers of the Church urged
their teaching "with all the resources of a penetrat-
ing logic, a dialectic skill, a grace of language, a
wealth of ornament and illustration, reminiscent of
classic Greece and Rome." [37]

[37] Hodgson, *Primitive Christian Education*, p. 123.

CHAPTER III

FATHERS OF THE EAST

THE era of Church history known as the age of the Fathers may be divided into two periods, the one prior, the other subsequent to the Council of Nicaea, A.D. 325. The Church Fathers may also be appropriately classified into the Fathers of the East and the Fathers of the West. The Fathers of the East wrote in Greek; the Fathers of the West, in Latin.[1] Many of them were educated in the public schools of the period, and some taught in them. They did not, however, owe their regard for learning wholly to the pagan schools they attended in their youth.

The more important Fathers of the East are St. Justin Martyr, Clement of Alexandria, Origen, St. Athanasius, St. Cyril of Jerusalem, St. Basil the Great, his brother St. Gregory of Nyssa, and their

---

[1] Migne in his great *Patrologia* applies the term "Fathers" to all Christian writers who possessed the notes of antiquity, orthodoxy, sanctity, and ecclesiastical approbation. The Fathers are, in the stricter sense of the term, the great champions of orthodox belief whose writings became the standard of truth.

intimate friend St. Gregory Nazianzen, St. John of Constantinople, also called St. John Chrysostom (golden-mouthed), Dionysius the Pseudo-Areopagite, and St. John of Damascus.

ST. JUSTIN MARTYR

St. Justin Martyr (c. 100–165) is the first of the Church Fathers to attempt a philosophy of Christian thought. He was a convert to the faith from the ranks of the philosophers. After his conversion he continued to wear the philosopher's gown, the academic dress of the wandering professional teacher of philosophy, traveling about, defending Christianity in his oral and written discourses. Born of pagan Greek parents in the pagan town of Flavia Neapolis, in Palestinian Syria, about the beginning of the second century, he was early instructed in the teachings of the current schools of philosophic thought. Contrasting these teachings with those of the prophets and of Christ, he concluded that the fullness of truth is found in Christianity. His conversion took place when he was about thirty years of age and probably at Ephesus. He taught and defended the Christian religion first in Asia Minor and later in Rome, where he conducted a catechetical school and where he was martyred about 165.[2]

[2] A. W. F. Blunt, editor, *The Apologies of Justin Martyr* (Cambridge: The University Press, 1911), p. x, note 1.

The three extant works of Justin of which the authenticity is assured are the two *Apologies* and the *Dialogue*.[3] The two *Apologies* are actually one because the second is a continuation of the first and dependent on it. The first *Apology*, which is the longer, is addressed to Antoninus Pius, his adopted sons (one of whom was Marcus Aurelius, the philosopher), the Roman Senate, and the people at large. In this work Justin gives a rather full exposition of Christian belief and practice, describing in detail the way the sacraments of baptism and the Holy Eucharist are conferred. He demands that Christian teaching be judged solely upon its merits. The aim of the *Apologies* is to reconcile Christianity with pagan science, and in the attempt to do this Justin makes the doctrine of the *Logos* the key of his philosophical position and insists on its excellence and truth.

The *Dialogue* is with Trypho, possibly Rabbi Tarpho, the most celebrated Israelite of that time.[4] Justin and Trypho meet in the colonnade of the gymnasium at Ephesus and discuss Christianity in the light of the Old Testament. The Law is first examined in relation to the Gospel; then the prophecies are analyzed to witness Christ as the Messiah; and the book closes with an appeal to the Jews to become Christians. The work may be said to be in

[3] Bardenhewer, *Patrology*, p. 52.
[4] *Ibid.*

part an account of real discussions between the author and learned Jews and in part an independent study of the claims of Christianity.

The writings of Justin lack for the most part artistic finish. In fact, they are at times very dull. It is only in the *Dialogue* that Justin shows an occasional flash of forceful expression.[5] He is not an original thinker, but he is a writer of respectable talent and shows that he is well-educated and well-read. His writings were freely used by his disciple Tatian and others, such as Athenagoras, Irenaeus, and Tertullian. His *Apologies* are not a technical treatise, but a plain statement of Christian truths as he understood them. He does not seek to formulate a system of Christian theology. The value of his writings lies in the historical position of their author in the development of Christian thought and in their record of the early efforts made to justify Christianity to the Graeco-Roman world.[6]

CLEMENT OF ALEXANDRIA

Titus Flavius Clemens, better known as Clement of Alexandria (c. 150–215 or 216), is regarded as the first of the Greek Fathers distinguished for learning.[7] In the judgment of St. Jerome he was the most

[5] *Ibid.*, p. 55.
[6] Blunt, *op. cit.*, pp. xi f.
[7] Sandys, *A History of Classical Scholarship*, I, 332.

learned of men.[8] Like Justin Martyr, he undertook to establish Christianity as a philosophy. In so doing he linked Christianity to Hellenism, maintaining that the best in Hellenic philosophy and ethics, especially Platonism, is in perfect agreement with Christian doctrine and practice. Clement, it is thought, was born of pagan parents about 150, very likely at Athens.[9] In his student days he wandered from one philosophical school to another in search of truth, never satisfied, until he came under the "transcendent powers" of Pantaenus, a converted Stoic, who was head catechist in the Alexandrian school. Of him Clement writes: "He, the true, the Sicilian bee, who gathered the spoil of the flowers of the prophetic and apostolic meadow, engendered in the souls of his hearers a deathless element of knowledge." [10] After his conversion, Clement traveled extensively through Asia Minor and Egypt making the acquaintance of other Christian teachers and receiving instruction from them.

When about thirty years of age he settled down in the city of Alexandria, became a presbyter of that Church, the colleague of Pantaenus in the work of the catechetical school and afterward his successor. He became headmaster of the school in the year 200,

[8] *Letter* 70; Migne, *Patr. lat.*, XXII, 667; *Nicene and Post-Nicene Fathers*, 2nd ser., VI, 150.
[9] Bardenhewer, *op. cit.*, p. 127.
[10] *Stromata*, I, 1; Migne, *Patr. gr.*, VIII, 699–702; *The Ante-Nicene Fathers*, II, 209.

remaining in that position for the next thirteen years, when he was forced to leave the city because of the persecution under Septimius Severus.

Pantaenus had introduced into the Alexandrian school a wider range of studies, but under the leadership of Clement and his brilliant young pupil and successor, Origen, a nobler scheme of Christian education was projected which made Alexandria the leading center of Christian learning until the fourth century. Clement was later associated at Caesarea with a former pupil, Alexander, the future bishop of Jerusalem, who in a letter to Origen written about 215 or 216 refers to Clement as then dead.

The educational theories and principles of Clement are best expressed in his *Exhortation to the Greeks, The Pedagogue,* and the *Stromata* or *Miscellanies.* This trilogy forms the contents of his *Introduction to Christianity.* It is necessary to read all three treatises to get a comprehensive view of his educational doctrine. The first work, in one book, deals largely with belief; the second, in three books, with the Christian ideal of conduct; and the third, in seven books, with human knowledge.

The *Exhortation to the Greeks* is similar in purpose to the *Apologies* of Justin the Martyr. It praises the superiority of Christianity over paganism by instituting comparisons between Christian practices and pagan rites, recalls the truth made known by the prophets, and points out that full truth is found in

[48]

Christ alone, the Logos, who calls all men to Himself. Many teachers among the Jews and the pagans have had glimpses of truth, but Christ is truth itself. Faith in Christ, then, is the cornerstone of knowledge.

The *Pedagogue* is definitely pedagogical and practical in tone. The emphasis in this work is on moral education. Clement is well aware that in a cosmopolitan environment such as was Alexandria, noisy with the din of philosophers, there was danger that the Christian student might pursue secular knowledge to the neglect of the all-important thing, the salvation of his soul. In other words, he cautions the student not to place secondary things first. The Instructor or Pedagogue is Christ. "Being practical, not theoretical, His aim is to improve the soul, not to teach, and to train up to a virtuous, not to an intellectual life." [11] Numerous passages dealing with discipline, wealth, companions, demeanor, and manners throw considerable light on Clement's doctrine and principles of moral education.

Physical training is rightly regarded by Clement as an integral part of a comprehensive education. Consequently the *Pedagogue* treats in detail matters pertaining to physical development: diet, sleep, dress, and recreation. The aim of physical education is the formation of a healthy body. Bodily exercises

[11] *Paedagogus*, I, 1; Migne, *ibid.*, 250. *The Ante-Nicene Fathers*, II, 209.

for women as well as for men are advocated, while music is advised as a form of recreation and as an aid to the cultivation of refinement and manners. Wrestling, ball playing, and walking are recommended for boys, and more active domestic employments for girls. Manual occupations, such as handling the hoe, turning the mill, and cutting wood, should be regarded not only as useful labor but also as suitable exercises for men.

The *Stromata* is the fullest exposition of Clement's educational doctrine. The work has no definite plan and repeats many of the ideas already brought forward in the other two treatises. The varied learning displayed in it reveals the encyclopedic knowledge of the author, showing that he was well acquainted with classical literature and the philosophical systems of the day. Clement is interested in all human learning, because human arts, he maintains, come from God as really as divine revelation. The Christian who wished to comprehend the truths of faith must be learned; the curriculum of Clement's catechetical school, which included grammar, rhetoric, logic, physics, geometry, astronomy, music, mathematics, medicine, and philosophy, prepared the student for a complete understanding of divine truth. Reason is made to serve faith. Philosophy becomes the handmaid of theology so that Clement's educational scheme bears close resemblance to the scholastic system of studies.

Although Clement relied on anthologies [12] for many of the references he uses, there is no doubt about his extraordinary learning.[13] He was quite at home with the best of the pagan professors in the university town of Alexandria, which had now begun to displace Athens as the center of culture. His catechetical school was a denominational college [14] in the midst of the Sarapeion, libraries, and schools, offering to catechumens and children a systematic course of religious instruction and to Christian or pagan students a higher education from the Christian standpoint. By the power of exact logic he discredited the arguments of pagan adversaries and in his writings attempted a scientific formulation of the revealed truths of Christianity. He integrated Christian truth with the products of Greek culture and, in so doing, suggested a use for the classics in the scheme of Christian education, which was effective in their preservation.[15] Despite the fact that he lacks technical precision in his theological statements, he is the courageous pioneer in the infant science of theology, and his humble beginnings have had a marked influence on the course of the theological science of later ages.

[12] Bardenhewer, *op. cit.*, p. 131.
[13] Sandys, *op. cit.*, p. 331.
[14] Bigg, *The Christian Platonists of Alexandria*, p. 42.
[15] Campbell, *The Greek Fathers*, p. 37.

ORIGEN

Origen (185 or 186–254 or 255) has already been mentioned as the distinguished pupil of Clement in the catechetical school of Alexandria, where he succeeded as head when he was only eighteen years old. He was a native of Egypt and, unlike his master, received a good religious training from Christian parents. His father died a martyr in the persecution of Severus and, as the family was deprived of any paternal inheritance, the youthful Origen was obliged to help support his mother and six brothers. This he did by becoming a teacher of grammar. His learning, enthusiasm, and ascetic life attracted the notice of Demetrius, bishop of Alexandria, who appointed him head of his school. Refusing to accept remuneration as catechist, he sold his library for a life pension of a mere pittance a day as a means of subsistence.[16] His ascetic zeal led him to an unreasonable act of mortification, self-emasculation.[17] For this reason Bishop Demetrius refused to ordain him priest. He was, however, later ordained by bishops Theoctistus of Caesarea and Alexander of Aelia, who, respecting the profound learning of the celebrated catechist, had already granted him permission as a layman to preach to the congregations in their

[16] Hodgson, *Primitive Christian Education*, p. 117.
[17] Bardenhewer, *op. cit.*, p. 136.

churches.[18] His own bishop now refused to accept him back in Alexandria. Thereupon he took up residence in Caesarea, opening a catechetical school there which soon eclipsed the fame of the Alexandrian institute. In the Decian persecution Origen was tortured and imprisoned as a Christian teacher, but apparently he survived that trial. However, as a result of the sufferings he endured, he died at the age of sixty-nine at Tyre, in 254 or 255.[19]

Origen is the first great scholar among the Church Fathers.[20] As a solid foundation of his theological studies, and in particular for its apologetic value, he undertook the study of Hebrew and prepared a monumental critical edition of the Bible containing six parallel columns in fifty large rolls of parchment, known as the *Hexapla*. In the first column he placed the Hebrew text, then the Hebrew text in Greek. Four other columns followed with the Greek versions of Aquila, Symmachus, the Septuagint, and Theodotion. Various incomplete versions were also included. The work, though not primarily one of textual criticism,[21] served to show the relation of the Septuagint to the Hebrew text and to the other Greek versions. The fifth column of the *Hexapla*, containing the revised Septuagint, still exists in a

[18] Duchesne, *The Early History of the Church*, I, 250.
[19] Bardenhewer, *op. cit.*, p. 137.
[20] Sandys, *op. cit.*, p. 341.
[21] Bardenhewer, *op. cit.*, p. 147.

Syriac version and is probably nearly all in existence.[22]

The most important of the doctrinal works of Origen is the *De principiis*. The original text, like that of his other doctrinal writings, has been lost. As we have the work today it is a translation made by Rufinus, who tells us in the preface that he has made a free paraphrase of certain parts of its four books. In this treatise Origen succeeded in achieving what Justin Martyr had a vague notion of and Clement had outlined. He Christianized Hellenism and, on the basis of the elements of the Creed, taught the catechumens a synthesis of fundamental principles of the Christian faith, which is the first summa of theology ever organized in the Church.[23] But the work was not free from error. It reveals traces of the teachings of his Neoplatonist master, Ammonius Saccas, and the influence of Gnosticism [24] which was masquerading as the true Christianity.

The grave mistake made by Origen was the same

[22] Bigg, *op. cit.*, p. 127.

[23] Campbell, *op. cit.*, p. 39. Cf. Martin Grabmann, *Die Geschichte der Scholastischen Methode* (Freiburg: Herdersche Verlagshandlung, 1909), I, 80.

[24] The sects of Gnosticism were many and its tenets contradictory. All its adherents were agreed that matter was not created by the Deity, but is in opposition to Him and is therefore the principle of evil. Gnosticism lingered on into the fifth century after receiving a severe blow from St. Irenaeus in the latter part of the second century in his refutation of the Gnosis, entitled *Adversus haereses*. This polemic is the first systematic account of the faith bequeathed by the apostles.

as that made by his predecessors. He relied too much
on philosophy. In the interpretation of the Scriptures he resorted to the allegorical method of exegesis, gave it a scientific basis, and evolved a theological
system in which salvation becomes a cosmic process
and both divine and human freedom are destroyed.

His apologetic work, *Contra Celsum*, is considered the most perfect of its kind in the primitive
Church.[25] In this treatise in eight books Origen displays the splendor of his erudition. It it quite unlike
any previous apology. The Christian philosopher
meets the pagan philosopher, Celsus, on his own
ground, following very closely the text of the attacks
made by his adversary against Christianity. With a
conviction of intellectual superiority he refutes his
arguments and objections one after the other upon
the basis of an appeal to reason.

The influence of Origen on his contemporaries
and later scholars is immeasurable. With the aid of
a corps of copyists supplied him by a rich friend, his
writings [26] were widely distributed and influenced

[25] Bardenhewer, *op. cit.*, p. 147.
[26] He was a voluminous writer. St. Epiphanius credited him
with six thousand books. St. Pamphilus attributed to him two
thousand titles, while St. Jerome reduces the number to eight
hundred. Antiquity has provided an anthology, the *Phocalia*,
drawn up about 382 by Basil the Great and Gregory Nazianzen, which offers a representative body of Origen's views
selected from the *De principiis*, *Contra Celsum*, commentaries,
and homilies. A scholarly edition of the work was edited by
Dr. J. Armitage Robinson, Cambridge, 1893.

all the outstanding Fathers of the East until the sixth
century, when his reputation suffered by reason of
the condemnations pronounced during the reign
of Justinian. His influence in the West was even
greater. Passages from his writings were introduced
into the Roman breviary, and his learning and sincerity were respected by Augustine, Bede, Bernard,
and Erasmus. His opinions are found reflected as
late as the seventeenth century in the Quietist doctrines contained in the educational theories of Féne-
lon and Madame Guyon.[27]

The fame of Origen's school at Caesarea spread
throughout the East. Here was offered a course of
studies similar to the scheme of Christian education
developed in the Alexandrian school. Theodore and
Athenodorus, scions of one of the best families in
Pontus, were educated in the school at Caesarea.
Both were excellent Latin scholars and were about
to proceed to the famous law center at Berytus to
study Roman jurisprudence when they were per-
suaded by Origen to take up philosophical studies
and examine the claims of Christianity. Both men
were converted from paganism and died as bishops
of the Church.[28] Theodore, who is known as St.
Gregory Thaumaturgus, expressed deep gratitude
to his illustrious teacher in a public panegyric pro-

[27] Bigg, *op. cit.*, pp. 278–301.
[28] Duchesne, *op. cit.*, p. 319.

nounced in the presence of his master for the excellent academic training he had received at his hands.[29]

In this discourse Gregory points out that the studies pursued in the school at Caesarea included dialectics, geometry, astronomy, physics, ethics, metaphysics, and theology. Dialectics was to exercise the minds of the students in separating the true from the false; geometry supplemented the training given in dialectics by habituating the pupils to the practice of clear demonstrations; astronomy enabled them to perceive the marvelous construction of the world, while physics served to give them a proper understanding of the works of God; philosophy, which taught the principles of ethics and metaphysics, was not limited to speculative thought, but was intended to influence the student in a practical way regarding the conduct of his life. All these branches of learning were preparatory to an understanding of theology, which teaches us the existence and nature of God. The aim of the latter subject was not to provide a complete comprehension of theology as a science but to make it the supreme guide to right living. The study of Christianity is the central interest in the curriculum of the school at Caesarea, and the different branches of learning constituting

[29] Gregory Thaumaturgus, *Oration and Panegyric Addressed to Origen;* Migne, *Patr. gr.,* X, 1051–1104; *The Ante-Nicene Fathers,* VI, 21–39.

a course of general culture form a series of successive steps leading to the interpretation of the Sacred Scriptures.

FATHERS OF THE GOLDEN AGE

The apologetic efforts of the Fathers of the second and third centuries prepared the way for the pre-eminence of the fourth century. The Christian educators of the fourth century like the Ante-Nicene Fathers were deeply concerned with the vital problems of Christianity, but their writings attained a literary excellence unapproached by their predecessors. The chief concern of the Church in the fourth century and at the same time a matter of intense interest to the state was the menace of the heresy of Arianism, which threatened the very life of Christianity. The foremost leader of orthodoxy in the Arian controversy is St. Athanasius. The Christology of St. Cyril of Jerusalem was expressed in the dignified and clear diction of his *Catecheses*. Other representatives of the century are the three Cappadocians, St. Basil the Great, St. Gregory of Nyssa, and St. John Chrysostom, an eminent authority on orthodox belief. The fifth century does not enjoy the pre-eminence of the fourth, but a remarkably strong and outstanding contribution of the new period appeared under the name of "St. Dionysius the Areopagite," which was to be widely used in subsequent times for orthodox sanction. It remained for St. John of Damascus after two centuries of compendiums and redactions to produce an adequate summary of the wisdom of his predecessors by which the best in the works of the Greek Fathers was bequeathed to posterity.

ST. ATHANASIUS

The talents and energy of St. Athanasius (c. 295–373) were absorbed in the Arian controversy.[30] His championship of the divinity of Christ stands out in strong contrast to the weak doctrinal ideas of his contemporary, Eusebius,[31] bishop of Caesarea, at whose house Arius took refuge, composing a defense of his position and writing songs for sailors, millers, and travelers illustrating his creed. Whereas Eusebius is the vacillating peacemaker, Athanasius

[30] Arianism, a heresy that arose in the fourth century, is called after the name of the heresiarch, Arius, who, brought up at Antioch and influenced by the doctrinal teachings of the well-known Lucian, attacked the mystery of the Trinity, asserting that Christ, the Son of God, was a creature. Polytheism, Platonism, and Gnosticism were embodied in the various teachings of Arius and his followers.

[31] Eusebius is the author of the great historical works, the *Chronicle* and the *Ecclesiastical History*, which have earned for him the title "Father of Church History." The *Ecclesiastical History* is a source-book of valuable materials rich in historical facts, documents, and quotations from a multitude of writings. The magnificent library founded by Pamphilus at Caesarea served Eusebius well in writing his *Ecclesiastical History*.

is a real Christian bishop of undaunted courage, the standard-bearer of the faith, ready to face exile for its preservation and to suffer the condemnations of the Empire and the Council that the truth might prevail.

Born at Alexandria about 295 [82] in the traditional atmosphere of philosophizing Christianity, Athanasius early came under the influence of Alexander, bishop of the city, who ordained him deacon, made him his secretary, and took him as his theological adviser to the Council of Nicaea in 325, where he was the dynamic instrument in the overthrow of Arianism. At the death of Bishop Alexander, Athanasius, because of the high esteem in which he had been held by Alexander and in recognition of the major role he had played at Nicaea, was at once acclaimed bishop of the city and was consecrated.[83] The next half-century of his life was marked by a series of five banishments from his see because of the hatred and intrigue of the Arians. Under Emperor Valens he was reinstated at Alexandria, where he lived the last seven years of his life at peace among the faithful and died in 373.[84]

Athanasius, though not a professional scholar, was a subtle dialectician [85] and a voluminous writer. His works include apologetical, dogmatic, exegetical,

[82] Bardenhewer, *op. cit.*, p. 253.
[83] Duchesne, *op. cit.*, II, 132.
[84] Bardenhewer, *op. cit.*, p. 254.
[85] Sandys, *op. cit.*, p. 349.

historical, and ascetical writings and pastoral letters. His two apologetic treatises, written before the Arian controversies and known to St. Jerome as *Adversus Gentes duo libri*, establish Christian monotheism and defend the mystery of the Incarnation against the objections of Jews and pagans.

The most important of his doctrinal works is the *Orationes IV contra Arianos*, written while he was in the deserts of Egypt during his third exile. In the first book the co-equality of the Son with the Father is taught; the second and third books cite scriptural texts in support of the Catholic doctrine.[36] The fourth book shows the personal distinction between the Father and the Son.

The most influential of the ascetical works of Athanasius is his *Life of St. Anthony*. While still under the direction of Bishop Alexander, he was attracted to the asceticism of the solitaries of Egypt and was influenced particularly by the great St. Anthony, the patriarch of monasticism, in his own

---

[36] Athanasius did not originate the famous term *homoousios*, "of the same substance." His writings show that he used the term sparingly. The word was current in Rome and officially used long before the Council of Nicaea took place. It is very probable that the use of the word was suggested to the Council by the Roman legates. Cf. *supra*, Duchesne, II, 121. The followers of Arius rallied round the term *homoiousios*, "of similar substance." There was only the difference of an "iota" in the two words, which is so small a letter in Greek that it is sometimes subscribed, but that "iota" meant that Christ was God or He was not and determined whether or not Christianity was to continue.

ascetical manner of living. In the Arian controversies Anthony had always stood firmly by his friend, Athanasius, and no ecclesiastical dissension was ever able to shake the high regard that the saint had for the courageous defender of Christianity. Athanasius looked upon St. Anthony's career as the model of a life consecrated to the service of God. In writing his biography he not only perpetuated the ideals of the famous solitary but contributed much in the East and West to the growing enthusiasm for the life of perfection. It is said that, when Athanasius visited Rome in 339, he was accompanied by two disciples of St. Anthony and recommended to Italy the ascetism of the Egyptian monks. The monastic life which soon sprang up in the provinces of the Western Empire under the inspiration of St. Anthony was a reaction against pagan culture; but under the influence of the community type of monasticism founded by St. Pachomius with Cassiodorus and St. Benedict as organizers, a movement was inaugurated that was to preserve pagan learning.

The influence of the *Life of St. Anthony* is revealed in the *Confessions* of St. Augustine, which show that it was a factor in his conversion. It was the source of inspiration for the monastic tales of St. Jerome and furnished material for a vast amount of literature and art that has endured from his day down to the present. Yet the significance of St. Athanasius as a world-figure is not owing to his place in the history of thought. He is the champion of revelation in an intellectual crisis. As a Christian philosopher, he placed theology above philosophy and also proved that, because of the primacy of the deposit of faith, there is no contradiction between reason and faith. This contribution was of sovereign importance to the future of civilization.[87]

St. Cyril of Jerusalem

St. Cyril of Jerusalem (c. 315–c. 386), like Athanasius, his contemporary, used his learning for the furtherance of the Christian faith by concentrating his attention on the intellectual side of Christian education. Both Fathers were witnesses to the claims of Arius and his party and shared identical views regarding the Catholic doctrines of the Trinity. In his famous catechetical instructions, Cyril prudently avoids using the disputed term *homoousios*, but his teachings are wholly sound and uncompromising with Arianism.[38]

The birthplace of St. Cyril is not known, but evidently he was educated at Jerusalem.[39] He was one of the priests of Bishop Maximus and enjoyed a great reputation for eloquence. Upon the death of his bishop he succeeded him in the see of Jerusalem. On account of the hostility of the Arians he was

[87] Campbell, *op. cit.*, pp. 52 f.
[38] Duchesne, *op. cit.*, II, 487.
[39] Bardenhewer, *op. cit.*, p. 271.

three times expelled from his see, ostensibly on the question of jurisdiction but actually because of his acceptance of the Nicene faith. His third exile lasted during the entire reign of Valens. After the Second Ecumenical Council of Constantinople in 381, at which he assisted, Cyril was recognized as a legitimate bishop and was permitted to return to Jerusalem. During the next five years he resumed the government of his diocese and died in the Holy City in 386.[40]

As a priest Cyril was appointed head catechist in the catechetical school at Jerusalem. While in this position he formulated the most important of his extant works, *Catecheses*, which is a series of catechetical lectures delivered in the season of Lent in 348.[41] They are a course of religious instructions presenting a complete body of doctrine. An introductory discourse, called the *procatechesis*, was given to the catechumens at a public service attended by a general congregation on the Sunday preceding the Lenten fast. This was followed by eighteen instructions, the first of which was addressed to the candidates for baptism the following Monday, and the eighteenth on the night of Good Friday.

The *procatechesis* emphasizes with a note of encouragement the importance of the grace which the catechumens are preparing to receive. The first *cate-*

[40] *Ibid.*
[41] Hodgson, *op. cit.*, p. 156.

chesis recapitulates the matter presented in the *pro-catechesis;* the next four treat of sin and repentance, baptism and its effects, Christian faith, and the nature of the virtue of faith respectively. The twelve *catecheses* that follow contain a full exposition of the Creed as it was recited by the candidate in the reception of the sacrament of baptism according to the ritual followed at Jerusalem.

The last five lectures, or mystagogical instructions addressed to the newly baptized, were delivered at the tomb of Christ on successive days beginning with the second day of Easter week. The first contains an explanation of the Christian mysteries based upon the last seven verses of the fifth chapter of St. Peter's First Epistle; the next two deal with the sacraments of baptism and confirmation; the fourth and fifth treat of Holy Communion and the Mass.

The *Catecheses* of St. Cyril are among the most precious treasures of Christian antiquity. The mystagogical lectures are especially valuable to the student of theology because they are a record of the doctrine and liturgy of the early Church. The first eighteen have a particular interest for the student of education because they are good models of instruction in general as well as in catechetics.

St. Cyril was a practical educator interested not only in the content of instruction but in the problem of presenting his subject matter. As the Jerusalem of his day was a populous city, inhabited by men of

many different races and degrees of culture, his class
of catechumens was a mixed audience. Probably the
slave, the soldier, the young man of the world, and
the public officer sat next to one another and were
instructed in the same group.[42] Cyril's method of
teaching was calculated to appeal to those acquainted
with domestic, military, and civil service as it was
to the man of practical affairs. He takes occasion to
refer to the mental effort necessary for an understanding of Christian doctrines and speaks of the
more simple among his auditors and of those who
are mature in thinking. While he is aware that the
illiterate, through lack of education, may not fully
grasp the truth, he observes that the learned may
confuse it by philosophical subtlety.[43] His lectures
are indicative of his literary ability and display a
richness of illustration, an orderly sequence of pres-
entation, and a remarkable clearness of exposition.
They appeal to the emotions as well as to the intel-
lect. Theological difficulties are solved by comparing
Christian truths to facts within his hearers' knowledge so that a careful elucidation is reached with
point and penetration.

THE THREE CAPPADOCIANS

In the second half of the fourth century, the
Church of Cappadocia claims intellectual leadership

[42] *Ibid.*, p. 169.
[43] *Ibid.*, pp. 178 f.

in that brilliant epoch of Christianity represented by St. Basil the Great, St. Gregory of Nyssa, and St. Gregory Nazianzen. The primacy which Alexandria enjoyed in the process of Christianizing Hellenism, owing to the vigorous and efficient labors of Clement, Origen, and Athanasius, now passed to Cappadocia under the direction of these three Christian teachers whose writings exerted a powerful influence not merely in the circles of the learned in the East but among the Latin Fathers of the West and among the scholastic educators of the medieval period. St. Gregory of Nazianzus tells us that, while the three of them were students in Athens, they knew but two streets in the city—one leading to the church and the other to the schools. Of the three, St. Gregory of Nyssa may be said to be the thinker, St. Gregory of Nazianzus the orator, and St. Basil the Great the practical Church prelate of action.[44]

St. Basil the Great

St. Basil (c. 331–379) so impressed his contemporaries with his powers of practical leadership that he was styled by them "the Great." Momentous problems, which involved the superiority of faith over reason, the refutation of Arian doctrines, the force of tradition in Catholic belief and practice, the place of the classics in the Christian educational scheme,

[44] Bardenhewer, *op. cit.*, p. 280.

the excellence of monastic life, were all ably handled by him. His treatment of them has merited for him the reputation of a distinguished homilist, of a worthy successor of Athanasius in defense of the true faith, of the father of Oriental monasticism, and of one of the greatest bishops of the Church. Born about 331 at Caesarea in Cappadocia [45] of good Christian parents in a family of ten children, Basil was given his early religious training by his grand-mother, Macrina, a deeply spiritual woman, and received his elementary education from his father, a rhetorician of high repute. His mother, Emmelia, was the daughter of a martyr; his brothers Gregory and Peter became bishops; his eldest brother, Nau-cratius, was a famous Christian jurist; his sister, Ma-crina, founded a religious community and is honored as a saint.

Basil was prepared academically in the best schools of Caesarea and Constantinople and finally at the University of Athens, where he formed an intimate friendship with Gregory of Nazianzus. After a bril-liant career as a university student, he returned to his native city to be a teacher and soon after was baptized by Dianius, metropolitan of Caesarea.[46] A journey through Egypt, Syria, and Mesopotamia at the suggestion of Eustathius, bishop of Sebaste, filled him with admiration for the mode of living of the

[45] *Ibid.*, p. 274.
[46] *Ibid.*, p. 275.

monks in these lands, whereupon he embraced a life of asceticism and founded a monastery in the valley of the Iris in Pontus.[47]

About 364 Basil was called from his Pontic cloister by Eusebius, the new metropolitan of Caesarea, who ordained him priest and prevailed upon him to remain in the episcopal city as his counsellor in dealing with the new crises in Arianism. Upon the death of the Archbishop, Basil was elected in his place to the great satisfaction of the illustrious Athanasius who felt he had someone to succeed him as the defender of the orthodox faith in the troublesome theological disputes then rending the Christian East.[48]

Basil was not only active in ecclesiastical legislation, but showed deep concern for the poor and afflicted. He opened hospices in his diocese where the sick poor were given medical treatment and the unskilled were industrially trained. His chief concern was the destruction of heresy, and his valiant stand against the imperial court itself, which was the main support of Arianism, prepared the East for the restoration of peace. Physically delicate, he lived less than half a century and died on January 1, 379, just at the dawn of what were to be better days.[49]

St. Basil is the patriarch of Oriental monasticism and the forerunner of St. Benedict. Eustathius of

[47] Duchesne, *op. cit.*, II, 306.
[48] *Ibid.*, p. 309.
[49] Bardenhewer, *op. cit.*, p. 276.

Sebaste had introduced the eremitical life into Asia Minor, but Basil favored a cenobitic system in which his monks should live under a common roof and eat and pray together. He agreed that it was very praiseworthy that monks should seek their own perfection, but at the same time he felt that they should be given opportunities to serve their fellow men. In the monastery organized by him in Neocaesarea the monks were urged to care for suffering humanity and conduct schools.

His Rule for monks was written in two parts: the larger and the shorter rules. Rufinus combined the two in his Latin translation of them under the title *Regulae sancti Basilii episcopi Cappadociae ad monachos*. As the Rules were intended to show monks how to live the religious life, the Bible was accepted as the true Rule. By means of questions and answers between the disciple and the master, St. Basil lays down principles for the guidance of superiors and subjects in their conduct based upon a verse or several verses of the Bible. The questions deal generally with the virtues of poverty, obedience, renunciation, and self-abnegation which the monks should practice and the vices they should avoid. The Basilian Rule was followed by some Western monasteries and still obtains in the Greek Church.

The principal theological work of St. Basil is his *De Spiritu Sancto*, which is a lucid exposition of the reconciliation of faith and reason and of the role of tradition in determining the contents of the Catholic faith. Although Basil is not an original theologian, he did the spade work in this treatise for the pronouncements laid down in the ecumenical decrees on the Holy Spirit by the Council of Constantinople in 381. An earlier work against Eunomius in three books reveals his expository powers in defense of the consubstantiality of the Son and the divinity of the Holy Spirit.

St. Basil's homily on the study of pagan literature is the treatise by which he is best known today. In his *Address to Young Men on the Right Use of Greek Literature*, he favored the judicious use of pagan literature in the education of Christian youth. The method to be followed in reading the ancient writers is the Christian method. Like Clement and Origen, he advocated the study of the classics as a preliminary training for the study of sacred science. His ideas on the right use of human learning are simplified by practical illustrations from nature. He observes that the tree bears fruit and leaves. The fruit represents the truth which is found in the Scriptures; the leaves are the ornaments of literature which adorn it. The bees extract honey from flowers, but not without discrimination. They take what is needed and let the rest go. The Christian student in like manner should take from pagan literature whatever is useful and leave the rest behind. In culling roses, we aim to avoid the thorns; so in reading the classical writers Christians should select what is beneficial and guard against what is contrary to Christian practice.[50] Basil further shows by many citations from Homer and other classical authors that ancient Greek literature contains many excellent precepts which elevate the mind and may be used to advantage in the training of Christian youth.[51]

The views expressed in this treatise affected early monastic education in the East and may have served to support the remarks of St. Jerome in his apologetic Epistle 70 concerning his fondness for quoting examples from secular literature and of St. Augustine in his *De doctrina christiana* on the usefulness of profane science.[52] They were certainly influential in the development of Christian education in the Middle Ages as is evidenced by the publication of twenty editions of the treatise by the close of the Early Renaissance period.[53]

St. Gregory of Nyssa

Little is known of the life of Basil's younger brother, St. Gregory of Nyssa (d. *ca.* 394), who was a profound philosopher and theologian yet far

[50] Edward R. Maloney, editor, *St. Basil the Great to Students on Greek Literature* (New York: American Book Company, 1901), pp. 20 f.

[51] *Ibid.*, pp. 21–24.

[52] Campbell, *op. cit.*, p. 61.

[53] *Ibid.*

less resourceful in action than his elder brother. His early literary training gave him a fondness for secular learning and prepared him for the calling of a teacher of rhetoric. The supervision that Basil had exercised over his education in early youth, together with the entreaties of Gregory of Nazianzus, influenced him to renounce the office of teacher and to embrace the clerical state. In 371 he was consecrated Bishop of Nyssa but was deposed from his see four years later because of violent opposition from the Arians of that place. He was forced to wander about from town to town until the death of Valens, when he returned to his people amid acclamations of great joy.[54] He was an outstanding champion of the orthodox faith in the Second Ecumenical Council at Constantinople and, in the year of his death, he was one of the principal theologians in a synod convened in the metropolitan city for the settlement of a controversy that had arisen among the bishops in the Church of Arabia. It is thought that he died about 394.[55]

The most extensive of his extant theological writings is his treatise against Eunomius in twelve books, which is a defense of St. Basil against the accusations of that heretic and a powerful refutation of Arianism. The most important of his theological works, one which has a special interest for the student of

[54] Bardenhewer, *op. cit.*, p. 295.
[55] *Ibid.*, p. 296.

catechetics and of pedagogy, is his *Oratio catechetica magna*. This "Great Catechism" in forty chapters displays his power of philosophical defense of Catholic doctrines against pagans, Jews, and heretics. The prologue of the work indicates that it was written to direct teachers in the different methods to be employed in the instruction of various classes of catechumens and observes how circumstances of the times demand that Christians make use of pagan culture and philosophy in order to understand better their opponent's point of view and to refute his opinions the more forcibly.[56] The contents of the work are especially noteworthy for their demonstration of the Christian doctrines of the Trinity,[57] the Incarnation of the Logos, the redemption of mankind,[58] and the application of the grace of redemption through the sacraments of baptism and the Eucharist.[59] The treatise reveals the author's scientific accomplishments, which he put to best use in the field of speculative thought.

The clear statement of purpose with which the "Great Catechism" opens indicates that Gregory not only made use of sound educational principles

[56] James H. Srawley, editor, *The Catechetical Oration of Gregory of Nyssa* (Cambridge: The University Press, 1903), pp. 1–6.

[57] *Ibid.*, pp. 6–19.

[58] *Ibid.*, pp. 52–123.

[59] *Ibid.*, pp. 123–153.

[74]

but that he was consciously doing so. The treatise was intended for catechists to help them to present in a rational form to catechumens the contents of the Christian revelation. This explains why the psychological rather than logical approach is in evidence throughout the work because its art and its appeal are pedagogical.[60]

As a philosopher Gregory of Nyssa is a disciple of Origen, whom he admired for his erudition and mental acumen. Many of his exegetical writings imitate the transcendental mode of exegesis of the Alexandrian doctor. In his efforts to rationalize the Christian faith, he betrays mental affinities with Origen, but his acceptance of him extends only so far as his writings are wholesome and useful.[61] His philosophical demonstrations of Christian dogmas are in a certain respect an anticipation of the Scholasticism of the Middle Ages. From his time on, Christian philosophy becomes, in regard to fundamental dogmas, what it was in the Middle Ages with few exceptions with reference to all doctrines, the handmaid of theology.[62] Gregory is always the conspicuous champion of orthodoxy. He is the first Christian mystic to construct a system of mysticism,

[60] John J. Hayes, *The Educational Principles in the Great Catechism of St. Gregory of Nyssa* (unpublished Master's thesis, The Catholic University of America, 1934), pp. 49 f.

[61] Duchesne, *op. cit.*, III, 28.

[62] Ueberweg, *History of Philosophy*, I, 328.

the basis of which is the extraordinary though limited power of the soul to know God because of the soul's reflection of the divine image.[63]

St. Gregory of Nazianzus

St. Gregory of Nazianzus (c. 330–389 or 390), like his school-fellow, Basil, was reared in a good Christian family under the direction of his saintly mother, Nona. He was born about 330, near Nazianzus in southwestern Cappadocia, and received his literary training in the best schools of Caesarea in Cappadocia, Caesarea in Palestine, Alexandria, and Athens.[64] It was at the University of Athens that he renewed his youthful friendship with Basil and studied rhetoric with him under the Christian teacher, Proaeresius, and the pagan, Himerius.[65] It was in the classroom here that he also had personally known Julian, the future emperor of Constantinople who became an apostate. When he was thirty years old he returned to his home, where he was baptized. Soon he joined Basil in his peaceful solitude in Pontus, assisting him in writing his rules for monks and editing with him an anthology of the works of Origen.

Gregory was ordained priest by his father, the

[63] Campbell, op. cit., p. 63.
[64] Bardenhewer, op. cit., p. 286.
[65] Sandys, op. cit., I, 349.

Bishop of Nazianzus, but because of scruples he fled back to the company of Basil only to return after serious reflection to his priestly ministrations and to write his *Apology for His Flight*, which eventually developed into a lengthy treatise on the priesthood. He was consecrated bishop by Basil, who was now metropolitan of Cappadocia, and acted as coadjutor at Nazianzus until the death of his father in 374, when he retired to a monastery at Seleucia. Five years later he was called to Constantinople by the scattered forces of the orthodox Catholics to re-organize the affairs of their Church. The religious zeal, remarkable learning, and marvelous eloquence which he displayed in his five famous discourses on the orthodox doctrine of the Trinity delivered in his humble chapel in the capital of the East won for him the title of "The Theologian." So widespread was his fame that St. Jerome, now a man advanced in years, came from his retreat in Syria and jour-neyed to Constantinople to listen to the preaching of Gregory and to receive instructions from him in the interpretation of the Scriptures.[66]

Gregory was declared the bishop of the capital city by the Fathers in the second general council of the Eastern bishops assembled by the Emperor The-odosius. On account of opposition and absurd dis-putes over his nomination to the metropolitan see, he resigned his post after a few months of service and

[66] Bardenhewer, *op. cit.*, p. 288.

returned to Nazianzus.[67] When the community of that city received a new pastor, he retired to the family estate of Arianzum, spending the remaining years of his ascetical life with his books. He died there probably about 389 or 390.[68]

The *Five Theological Orations* of Gregory make him the representative exponent of the tradition of Christian faith toward the close of the fourth century. Communion with him is the test of orthodoxy of all subsequent theologians dealing with the Trinity. His orations nourished later theological writers in the East, notably St. John of Damascus who is heavily indebted to him.[69] The genius of Gregory does not lie in independent speculation but rather in the lucid exposition of the unchanging faith amid the changing circumstances of his day.

The first of his works, *Apology for His Flight*, is the model of numerous similar treatises which followed subsequently on the priesthood. The *De sacerdotio* of St. John Chrysostom and the *Regula pastoralis* of Pope Gregory the Great reveal the influence of this remarkable apologetic oration.[70]

For the student of educational history the two invectives against the Emperor Julian, *Orationes invectivae contra Julianum Inperatorem*, have a special significance. The orations were composed after the

[67] Duchesne, *op. cit.*, II, 347.
[68] Bardenhewer, *op. cit.*, p. 288.
[69] Grabmann, *op. cit.*, p. 87.
[70] Campbell, *op. cit.*, p. 65.

death of Julian and probably were never delivered publicly.[71] In his accusations against the apostate emperor, Gregory shows his bitter opposition to Julian's law of 362 which excluded Christians from the cultivation of secular literature. Gregory proclaims his high regard for rhetorical skill just as St. Basil had declared his admiration for the culture of the pagan poets and philosophers. He protests strongly against this interdict which aims to curtail Christian liberty in education. He calls upon everyone who shares his views about the higher education of Christians to share with him his indignation against the efforts to deprive them of it. He glories in the long years of labor he has spent in acquiring excellence in polite letters, for learning is more to be desired than earthly riches or noble birth. Next to the joys of eternal life, he holds literature most dear to him on earth.[72]

Many of the numerous poems of Gregory written toward the end of his life were intended to compensate in some measure for the loss of the poetic creations of the classic Greek authors. He has been styled "the Poet of Eastern Christendom," and compared to the great master, Dante, for his power of clothing deep theological doctrines in poetic garb. The longest of his poems, *De vita sua*, may have in-

[71] Bardenhewer, *op. cit.*, p. 289.

[72] C. W. King, *Julian the Emperor*. An English translation of the *Orationes invectivae*. (London: George Bell and Sons, 1888), p. 67.

fluenced the formation of St. Augustine's *Confessions*. His epitaphs have been translated into English as late as the nineteenth century, and some of his poems have been paraphrased by Cardinal Newman.[73]

"GREAT TEACHER OF THE EARTH"

The best known of the Greek Fathers is St. John Chrysostom (344 or 347–c. 407), who was styled, by his fellow Antiochians, "Great Teacher of the Earth." Born at Antioch, probably about 344 or possibly in 347,[74] he received an admirable Christian training from his pious mother, Anthusa. Despite the dangers to morals and religion that prevailed in the state academies, he was permitted to attend the best schools in his native Antioch, then the second city in the Eastern Empire, where he was a pupil of the pagan, Libanius, the most celebrated rhetorician of that period.[75] His natural genius so impressed the famous orator that on his deathbed, according to the story, he expressed a wish that his Christian disciple might succeed him in the chair of eloquence.[76]

After a short but brilliant legal career, Chrysostom made a study of Christian doctrines in the household of Meletius, bishop of Antioch, and was

[73] Campbell, *op. cit.*, pp. 65 f.
[74] Bardenhewer, *op. cit.*, p. 347.
[75] Sandys, *op. cit.*, I, 350.
[76] Duchesne, *op. cit.*, II, 477.

baptized by him about 369. Four years later he was nominated for the episcopal office, but he fled from the honor, later justifying his action in the six splendid books of his dialogue *De sacerdotio*.[77] Upon the death of his mother, his admiration for monastic solitude led him to the mountains south of Antioch where he passed six fruitful years in theological study and prayer. His excessive ascetic practices weakened his health and he was forced by sickness to return to Antioch. There he was immediately ordained deacon and five years afterward was raised to the priesthood by Flavian, the successor of Meletius. As a priest of the Church of Antioch he was an eminent pulpit orator. It was here that he delivered a series of extempore orations known as the twenty-one *Homilies on the Statues*, which were occasioned by the overthrow of the imperial statues on account of a riotous demonstration against new taxes imposed by Theodosius.[78]

The fame of Chrysostom had spread to the capitals of the Byzantine Empire, and in 397 he was summoned from Antioch to succeed Nectarius as archbishop of Constantinople. During the remaining decade of his life he was the victim of his zealous efforts to impress the faithful with the duties and responsibilities of Christians and of his determination to bring about needed reform among the clergy and

[77] Bardenhewer, *op. cit.*, pp. 323 f.
[78] Duchesne, *op. cit.*, p. 478.

the aristocracy. Twice he incurred the indignation of the revengeful Eudoxia, into whose hands rapidly passed the control of imperial authority. Once he was banished by her from the capital, but recalled. A lonely mountain village named Cucusus, on the borders of Cilicia and Armenia, was selected by the revengeful Empress as the place of his second exile. The letters sent him and the visits paid him here prompted her partisans to send him to Pityus, a most inhospitable spot at the foot of the Caucasus near the eastern extremity of the Euxine, far removed from roads of communication. Taken by two brutal guards across the mountains of Pontus, he ended his exile near Comana, where he died in a humble country oratory dedicated to a local martyr, St. Basiliscus, on September 14, 407.[79] His last words were the motto of his life, "Glory be to God for all things, Amen." When his body was brought to Constantinople, the young Emperor Theodosius II, the son of Arcadius and Eudoxia, bowed low over the remains of the martyr and asked God's forgiveness for the injustice done by his parents to the great saint who had spent himself in the service of the pulpit and archiepiscopal chair of Constantinople.[80]

The literary legacy of Chrysostom includes extensive exegetical homilies, numerous sermons

[79] Bardenhewer, *op. cit.*, p. 329.
[80] Duchesne, *op. cit.*, Vol. III. Translated into English by Claude Jenkins, p. 271.

on miscellaneous subjects, apologetic and ascetico-moral writings, and copious letters. His works fill eighteen volumes of Migne (*Patr. gr.*, XLVII–LXIV). His most read tractate, *De sacerdotio*, has gone through innumerable editions and was a stimulating source of reference for Pope Gregory in producing the first treatise on pastoral theology, the *Regula pastoralis*.

In his exegetical methods Chrysostom shows the effects of his training in the Antiochian school. Unlike the practice in the school at Alexandria of discovering allegorical interpretations, the school at Antioch labored to discover the grammatical sense of a passage of Scripture before undertaking to expound it. Chrysostom disclaimed allegory except where it was evident that the Sacred Writings revealed allegorical intention. He has a genius, whether as exegete or pulpit orator, in treating of moral themes, for bringing the thought of Holy Scripture into touch with the life of his own time and the life of every age.[81] In his hands the Scriptures are the source of living progress in all branches of religious life. Because he was not interested in metaphysical speculations, he makes little use of philosophical terms, yet he was invoked in his own and later centuries in both East and West by all defenders of the faith.

Chrysostom is by universal consent the *Doctor*

[81] Swete, *Patristic Study*, p. 104.

Eucharistiae. His numerous clear and detailed statements concerning the Blessed Sacrament form a complete exposition of the teaching of the Catholic Church on the doctrine of the Real Presence.[82] The expressions he uses to explain the change which takes place through the words of the priest in the Consecration of the Mass are a confirmation of the doctrine of transubstantiation.

As a writer on pedagogical matters, St. Chrysostom is superior to all other ecclesiastical authors of the patristic period. His educational theories and principles are best formulated in his treatise *De liberis educandis.* This work was edited for the first time at Paris in 1656, through the industry of Father Francis Combesis of the Dominican Order who came upon the manuscript. Two years later it was translated into English by John Evelyn, who dedicated the publication of the text to his two brothers in order to comfort them on the death of their children.[83] Evelyn calls this treatise the Golden Book of St. John Chrysostom. Within the twenty-four pages of the English translation, the education of the child from infancy to maturity is outlined. Within the outline are to be found all the essential elements of a sound education in accordance with Christian moral standards. The keynote of the educational

---

[82] Fortescue, *The Greek Fathers,* pp. 126 f.
[83] William Upcott, *The Miscellaneous Writings of John Evelyn* (London: Henry Colburn, 1825), pp. 112 f.

philosophy of the author is sounded in the opening part of the treatise, when he cautions the father about becoming overindulgent toward the child and exhorts him to bring up a champion for Christ by instructing him in good principles from his tender years.[84] The real beginnings of Christian education are made in the home.

And as in a wrestling place, before they play the prize, they daily exercise with their companions, that making their party good with them, they may the more easily vanquish their antagonists: so should a child be educated at home.[85]

The theory that all learning comes through the senses was well known to Chrysostom. He compares the soul of the child to a newly built city whose gateways are the senses of seeing, hearing, and smell, together with touch, all of which must be carefully guarded so that evil influences may be prevented from entering.

The child's nurse and attendants must, therefore, be of good morals. His teacher should be carefully selected because he shares in large part in the formation of the child's character. Parental example is a powerful educational factor. Corporal punishment is to be used sparingly so that the child may be accustomed "to fear the rod, not always to feel

[84] *Ibid.*, p. 114.
[85] *Ibid.*, p. 129.

it." The actions of children are to be guided by the direction of their parents, who must be solicitous much as sculptors are concerned about the making of wonderful statues.

So you also, like so many statuaries, bend all your endeavor, as preparing these admirable statues for God, take away that which is superfluous, add that which you find wanting: consider every day how they abound in natural endowments, that you may timely augment them: what natural defects you espy, that you may accordingly abate them: but with all sedulity, and above all things, be careful to exterminate unseemly speeches, for this custom begins extremely to infect the minds of youth; yea, and before he have essayed it, teach him to be sober, to be vigilant and assiduous in his devotions, and upon whatsoever he saith or doth to put the seal upon it.[86]

There is scarcely any phase of education in relation to child development that is not touched upon in Chrysostom's treatise. He insists that "idle fables" should not be told children and suggests in their stead stories from the Bible which will help to develop their moral judgment. He elaborates on this suggestion by recounting the biblical narratives of Cain and Abel, Jacob and Esau, and points out in detail how scriptural stories form a vehicle for moral training and religious instruction.[87] In like manner children should be given the names of saints rather

[86] *Ibid.*, p. 115.
[87] *Ibid.*, pp. 120 f.

than be called by the names of their ancestors, in order that they may "court the affinity of the righteous" rather than that of progenitors.[88]

The latter part of Chrysostom's treatise is devoted to a practical discussion of sex instruction for the youth who if he is destined to a secular life must be carefully directed until he is married. In his treatment of young men who are approaching maturity after the age of fifteen he advises that their thoughts be kept pure and clean through the creation of wholesome interests by legitimate relaxation, elevating conversation, good books, sound poetry, and contemplation of the beauties of nature,[89] but above all through the practice of self-denial by the cultivation of prayer. They should learn of the praise which is accorded men of self-control and of the honor in which men of good moral character are held by the members of the community.[90] Because of the dangers that threaten adolescents, Chrysostom discourages their attendance at the theater, warns them against mixed bathing, denies them the services of a young maid, and condemns effeminacy.

The education of girls is practically the same as that of boys. Mothers are requested to reprove their daughters who show a liking for extreme and luxurious fashions in dress. Such taste is often the mark

[88] *Ibid.*, p. 125.
[89] *Ibid.*, p. 127.
[90] *Ibid.*, p. 133.

of an undesirable woman in society. Since young women are believed to be proud and haughty, they must be properly instructed and disciplined by their mothers so that the results of their training may be as fruitful as that of boys.[91]

Throughout his treatise Chrysostom emphasizes the importance of the home training of the child, shows a sympathetic understanding of child psychology, touches upon the subject of vocational guidance, and outlines a direct training for citizenship. He urges the cultivation of the powers of observation, applies the doctrine of imitation, and regards the principle of emulation as an important incentive to effort. His great concern is the development of a sound Christian character by means of religious and moral training in the earnest effort to bring up "a philosopher, and a champion, and a citizen of heaven."

Similar ideas on the necessity of Christian training for children are to be found in his sermons and letters. His preference for monastic schools because of the dangers to Christian youth in the public schools of the period is expressed in his *Adversus oppugnatores vitae monasticae; ad patrem fidelem.*

St. John Chrysostom has influenced the world of his own day and of later generations deeply and tangibly. Within his own lifetime, while he was still a young priest, his superior talents were recognized

[91] *Ibid.,* p. 137.

by St. Jerome, who gave him deserved notice in his *De viris illustribus*. The Pelagian heretics, who in their controversy with St. Augustine on original sin first translated him into Latin, unwittingly won for him the approval of the greatest of the Latin Fathers, which gave his works assurance of Western diffusion. John Cassian, whose personal influence and writings contributed to the spread of monasticism in the West, was a favorite disciple of Chrysostom at Constantinople. Cassiodorus, who inaugurated in his monastery the practice of copying manuscripts, included treatises of Chrysostom among the works to be reproduced. Educators of the Carlovingian period —Alcuin, Rhabanus Maurus, and Hincmar of Reims —found in him a stimulating source of information. His influence on the Schoolmen of the thirteenth century is even more marked. The great doctors of that glorious period of Scholasticism—St. Albertus Magnus, St. Thomas Aquinas, and St. Bonaventure —appealed to his authoritative witness by quoting passages from him frequently.[92] During the age of the Classic Renaissance twenty-seven of his works were edited by Erasmus. The educational treatises written during this period by the Catholic humanists show a dependence on Chrysostom as the outstanding Christian educator of the fourth century. Although Luther underestimated him, Melanchthon, who was better qualified as a scholar to judge

[92] Campbell, *op. cit.*, pp. 73 f.

him, urged his study. So compelling was the force of his sanction that the Protestants both in Germany and in England attempted to claim him as their own. From the ninth century on there is abundant evidence of the efforts of educators to appropriate his authority. Even to this day his method of sex instruction is considered superior to any other theory advanced on the subject in the history of education.[93]

LATER GREEK FATHERS

The golden age of the Fathers of the East was followed by an era of decline in Christian literature. Later theological writers among the Greeks have not the excellence, intellectual and stylistic, that characterized the works of Chrysostom and the Cappadocians.[94] After the middle of the fifth century there is little creative vigor in Greek theology. Any erudition that is displayed henceforth in ec-

[93] Eby and Arrowood, *The History and Philosophy of Education Ancient and Medieval*, p. 605.

[94] St. Cyril of Alexandria and Theodoret are intellectual exceptions. Cyril's precise definitions of the orthodox belief give his writings a solidity and strength of conviction which command admiration. His refutation of Nestorianism and other dogmatic treatises, his powers as an exegete of the mystical school, and his important collection of letters render his theological works of permanent value. Theodoret, a learned adversary of Cyril, is an outstanding Graeco-Christian apologist. He had done excellent work as exegete and historian. His letters are valuable for the history of dogma and for the general Church history of the fifth century. Cf. *supra*, Henry B. Swete, pp. 105–10.

clesiastical literature is to be found in the form of *florilegia* which had been gathered from the writings of superior minds of former days. The field of hymnography alone gives evidence of the literary force of the golden age.[95] The two exceptions in this period of universal mediocrity are the remarkable series of writings which has been ascribed to the end of the fifth or the beginning of the sixth century, under the pseudonym of Dionysius the Areopagite, and the *Fountain of Wisdom* of John of Damascus.

DIONYSIUS THE PSEUDO-AREOPAGITE

At the beginning of the sixth century citations began to appear from a number of theological works which, it is agreed, are the compositions of a single writer who until recent times was supposed to have been Dionysius the Aeropagite, the judge of the Areopagus converted to Christianity by the preaching of St. Paul and later the first bishop of Athens. Critical scholarship has determined that the author did not belong to the times of the apostles, but at the very earliest to the latter half of the fifth century, and that he probably was a native of Syria.[96]

This series of writings of the Pseudo-Dionysius forms a collection of four treatises and ten letters. The first treatise, the most important in scope and

[95] Bardenhewer, *op. cit.*, p. 529.
[96] *Ibid.*, pp. 539 f.

contents, treats in thirteen chapters of the divine
names, illustrating through them the nature and
attributes of God. The second treatise deals in fifteen chapters with the heavenly hierarchy which
consists of the nine orders of angels whose work on
earth is continued through the administration of the
sacraments by the priests of the Church. The third
treatise in seven chapters describes the gradation of
ecclesiastical authority and indicates a parallelism
between the Church on earth and the heavenly
world. The fourth treatise on mystical theology in
five chapters contends that, although it is impossible
for human nature to comprehend the divine nature,
there are certain guiding principles which demonstrate to man his mystical union with his Creator.
Most of the ten letters are very short. Their contents
are largely theological, giving supplementary information on Christian doctrine discussed in the four
treatises, offering practical suggestions for dealing
with infidels and sinners and, among other points,
stressing the importance of the virtues of humility
and mildness.

Although the name and birthplace of the author
of this series of famous writings are unknown, the
remarkable fact about them is that they attained a
circulation and exercised a constructive influence on
Western theological science in subsequent centuries
unequaled by any other work of the Greek Patristic. They won authority among orthodox and he-

retical Christians alike, and were appealed to for confirmation of the truth of mutually conflicting doctrines. In their attempt to Christianize the Neoplatonist philosophy and to harmonize mystical and dogmatic theology, they became a model and a source for mystic, scholastic, ascetic, exegetical, and liturgical writers.

From the seventh century onward the popes were familiar with these works. Gregory the Great, Paul I, and Adrian I are distinguished channels through which they were introduced to the West and circulated among Christian rulers. In the ninth century, the Greek Emperor Michael, the Stammerer, presented a copy of them to Louis the Pious, while Hilduin, abbot of St. Denis, had them translated into Latin. The interest of Hilduin in this translation led to the belief that the author of them was identical with St. Denys of Paris, the national saint of France. Other Latin translations followed. The Irish monk, John Scotus Erigena, was commissioned by Charles the Bald to make a better translation of these writings, which appeared about 858. In the twelfth century John Saracenus and in the thirteenth Robert Grosseteste also made translations of them. During the period of glory of Scholasticism the great Schoolmen, Hugh of St. Victor, Peter Lombard, Alexander of Hales, St. Albertus Magnus, Vincent of Beauvais, St. Bonaventure, and St. Thomas Aquinas adopted theses and arguments from the writings of the Pseudo-Dionysius. So heavily yet critically did the Angelic Doctor draw from them that Abbé Darboy, later archbishop of Paris, who translated the works of the Areopagite into French about the middle of the nineteenth century, has observed that if these writings were lost they could be reconstructed from the numerous citations from them to be found in St. Thomas' works.[97] With the decay of Scholasticism came also the decline of the far-reaching influence of Pseudo-Dionysius, but not before he had played a major role in the treatises of the cardinal educators of the Middle Ages.

St. John of Damascus

It was the mighty intellectual leader, John of Damascus, in the eighth century who gathered into a systematic form the scattered teaching of earlier theologians. The exact dates of the birth and death of this last of the Greek Fathers are unknown.[98] He was born toward the end of the seventh century of a native Christian family in Damascus. His father was an excellent man who held an office in the revenue department under the Mohammedan government. Deeply concerned with works of charity, he used much of his wealth in redeeming Christian captives,

[97] Campbell, *op. cit.*, p. 81.
[98] Bardenhewer, *op. cit.*, p. 583.

among whom was a learned Sicilian monk by the name of Cosmas, who later became his son's tutor, instructing him and his adopted brother in all the sciences of the day, but especially theology.[99]

Upon the death of his father, John accepted the hereditary position in his family as minister of the revenue department in the service of the Caliph, but about 730 he resigned his post and with his brother entered the monastery of St. Saba at Jerusalem. He was ordained priest by John V, patriarch of Jerusalem, who wished him to take up his duties in that church, but St. John returned to his monastery where he died about the middle of the eighth century after devoting his remaining years to ascetic practices and to ecclesiastical learning.[100]

The most famous of the writings of St. John of Damascus is his great compendium, *Fountain of Wisdom*, which is the standard theological work of Eastern Scholasticism and holds to this day a position in the orthodox East analogous to the *Summa* of Aquinas in the West.[101] It is divided into three parts. The first, known as *Dialectica*, contains not only a treatise on logic but also a course of Aristotelian ontology. The second part is a history of heresies. Most of it is a duplication of the *Panarion* of Epi-

[99] Fortescue, *op. cit.*, pp. 210 f.
[100] Bardenhewer, *op. cit.*, p. 583.
[101] Swete, *op. cit.*, p. 113.

phanius with concluding paragraphs about Moham-
medans and the aberrations of Iconoclasts and other
later heretics. In the third part is his most important
work, *De fide orthodoxa,* which was divided in the
West into four books, probably in imitation of Peter
Lombard's four books of *Sentences.*[102] The first
book in nineteen chapters treats of God; the second
in thirty chapters of creation, angels, demons, man,
and divine Providence; the third in twenty-nine
chapters, of the doctrine of the Incarnation and its
consequences; and the fourth in twenty-seven chapters deals with a variety of topics arranged with little
attention to systematic order, such as: the glory of
God the Son; the sacraments of baptism and the
Eucharist; the veneration of saints, relics, and images; the canon of the Scriptures; the problem of evil
in the world; and the last things.

In philosophy, St. John is a confirmed Aristotelian. His *Dialectica* includes a great deal of metaphysics and psychology. The basic idea in his
metaphysics is Aristotle's distinction between *actus*
and *potentia,* which also finds familiar use in the
writings of St. Thomas Aquinas. In psychology he
distinguishes four internal faculties, viz., imagination, memory, reason, and will. In theology he discusses three of the five scholastic proofs for the
existence of God, arguing from motion, from the
conservation of the world, and from the order of

[102] Bardenhewer, *op. cit.,* p. 584.

nature, while his demonstrations of the attributes of God are current in the schools of the West.[103]

The distinction and influence of John of Damascus is not limited to his *Summa*. He was a poet of rare merit. The most famous of all his hymns are the odes of his *Golden Canon* for Easter Sunday. When sung in the Byzantine Church together with the sudden lighting of the candles, they make an impression as great as that of the Gloria and bells and organ at the first Easter Mass in the Latin rite.[104] The weight of scholarly opinion still favors St. John as the author of the tale of Barlaam and Josaphat, the most popular romance during the Middle Ages.[105] The moral contents of this Christianized version of the Indian story of Buddha gained so great vogue that it was translated into most of the European languages. It supplied medieval playwrights with material for miracle plays and furnished episodes and apologies to romancers, poets, and preachers.

As a theologian, St. John of Damascus wrote on every question of theology that had been raised up to his time, yet his only original contribution to this science was his defense of the veneration of images, in three discourses written in opposition to the iconoclasm of Leo the Isaurian. As indicated by the title, *Fountain of Wisdom,* of his encyclopedia of

[103] Fortescue, *op. cit.*, pp. 229–31.
[104] *Ibid.*, p. 236.
[105] Campbell, *op. cit.*, p. 84.

Christian theology, he relied chiefly on the solutions of his predecessors, the Post-Nicene Fathers,[106] in matters dogmatic and exegetical; yet so eruditely and accurately did he assemble the wisdom of these ecclesiastical authorities that the scholars of the following centuries in both East and West are indebted to him for the eminence of his sources. When part of the *De fide orthodoxa* was translated into Latin in the middle of the twelfth century by the distinguished jurist Joannes Burgundio, an envoy of Barbarossa in the East, it was readily accepted by Western theologians. Peter Lombard found in it helpful suggestions for the arrangement of the matter of his *Sententiae*, and St. Thomas regarded it as a thesaurus of tradition in the comprehensive scheme of scholastic education. In his efforts to apply the Aristotelian system of logic to Christian theology, St. John became, through these two eminent Scholastics, an authoritative influence among the Schoolmen of the West.[107]

[106] Karl Krumbacher, *Geschichte der byzantinischen Literatur* (München: C. H. Beck'sche Verlagsbuchhandlung, 1897), 2nd ed., p. 70.

[107] Sandys, *op. cit.*, I, 392.

CHAPTER IV

FATHERS OF THE WEST

THE Fathers of the West are the disciples of the Fathers of the East. They differ markedly from their Greek masters, however, in intellectual temperament. The Byzantine mind is fundamentally theological and, although the Fathers of the West are not opposed to speculation and dialectic, their writings show a distinctly Latin spirit, a preoccupation with practical and moral problems. The Latin Fathers improved upon what they learned from their Greek predecessors and contemporaries and found new truth for themselves.

Up to the end of the second century, the Church was faithful to Hellenism. Until then, Greek was probably the chief medium of expression for Christian thought in the West, especially in Rome.[1] The early Christian writings in Latin were humble translations from the Greek Bible for the use of the Latin faithful who had little acquaintance with the Greek. With the turn in the tide of conflict between pagan-

[1] De Labriolle, *History and Literature of Christianity*, p. 5.

[99]

ism and Christianity in favor of the latter, the new religion continued to gain in the number and influence of its converts. Previously in the West, most converts to the faith had been of the lower classes; but now lawyers, professional teachers, and government officials became Christians. The Latin Church now possessed polished intellects imbued with classical culture and ready to set forth their faith. The glory of giving birth to the earliest of the famous Fathers of the West was reserved for the city of Carthage. Chief among these are Tertullian, Cyprian, and Lactantius. These men of letters were formed in the best schools of Roman Africa, but they eclipsed their pagan rivals by the serious purpose of their writings, which evinced a deep sense of conviction.[2]

The outstanding figures during the age of the great doctors in the West are St. Hilary, St. Ambrose, St. Jerome, and St. Augustine. The first three knew Greek well and their works reflect an intimate acquaintance with the Fathers of the East. Augustine, too, reveals the influence of a considerable Greek Christian inheritance. St. Hilary was exiled to the East, and there studied the doctors of the Greek Church. St. Jerome settled in Bethlehem and while in the Orient benefited by the personal instruction of Gregory of Nazianzus. St. Ambrose and St. Augustine remained in the West but, through

[2] *Ibid.,* p. 10.

continual intellectual relations with the East, by correspondence and study were nourished on the opinions of the Greek Fathers.[3]

St. Augustine, the last and greatest of the Christian writers in the golden age of the Latin Fathers, dominated the whole history of the Church from the beginning of the fifth century. As the great theological authority, he became the foremost teacher of the Middle Ages. His deep penetration into the subject of divine grace in its relation to human acts earned for him from all later generations the title of "Doctor of Grace." St. Hilary and St. Ambrose were the worthy Latin forerunners of Jerome in the work of expounding portions of the Scriptures. St. Hilary in his exposition of the words of the Bible aims at avoiding the misuse of literal interpretation and allegory. St. Ambrose, while seeking for mystic meanings in scriptural passages, is largely concerned with their moral application to the duties of men.[4]

Whether bishops, like Hilary, Ambrose, and Augustine; priests, like Tertullian and Jerome; or laymen, like Arnobius and Lactantius, the Latin Fathers regarded their mission as writers in the light of a service to Christianity. Some of them served the Church by combating heresy and expounding orthodox teaching, others by studying the problem of the

[3] Bardy, *The Christian Latin Literature of the First Six Centuries*, p. 70.
[4] Laistner, *Thought and Letters in Western Europe*, p. 44.

use of secular literature, and defending the rules of
Christian life.

TERTULLIAN

Quintus Septimius Florens Tertullianus (160–
240) was born at Carthage of pagan parents about
the year 160.[5] The son of a centurion in the proconsular service, he was well instructed in all the
branches of learning of his time and became equally
proficient in the studies of literature and law. He
wrote with wonderful facility in Latin and Greek
and had an extensive acquaintance with the teachings of the great philosophers, besides giving evidence of a knowledge of physiology and the natural
sciences. His remarkable attainments in law characterized the general tone of his writings, and his
extraordinary ability is apparent when he displays
the logic and subtlety of his legal mind.[6]

Turning from his life of paganism, which was far
from exemplary in conduct, he was baptized a Christian, certainly before 197, and ordained a priest,
whereupon he entered into a period of pastoral
activity and literary accomplishments in the service
of the Catholic Church which terminated five years
later when he joined the sect of the Montanists.[7] His

[5] Bardenhewer, *Patrology*, p. 179.
[6] De Labriolle, *op. cit.*, pp. 57 f.
[7] Bardenhewer, *loc. cit.*

immoderate zeal led him to believe that the virtues
which he found lacking among his brethren were
practiced by the partisans of Montanus, who advocated withdrawal from the world, and maintained
the unlawfulness of second marriages and the im-
pending second advent of Christ.[8]

Tertullian later withdrew from the Montanists
and founded a new sect of his own whose members
were known as Tertullianists. They existed at Carthage up to the time of Augustine, who is credited
with having reconciled the last adherents of the
party to the Catholic Church.[9] The last years of
Tertullian's life were spent in using his natural
gifts in writing pamphlets, violent and paradoxical,
against his brethren whom he defended so elo-
quently and vigorously in his earlier works. Ecclesiastical writers do not indicate that he ever repented
of his folly. He died unnoticed by his countrymen
about 240.[10]

The writings of Tertullian are controversial.
Some of them are in defense of the faith against the

[8] The Montanists originated in Phrygia about 172. Their
founder was Montanus, who claimed to be a prophet. In his
apostolate, two women, Maximilla and Priscilla, were associated. Montanism was a belief in the advent of the Holy Spirit
incarnate in the person of Montanus. His prophetesses were
also regarded as fulfilling the mission of the Paraclete. Its
adherents regarded the precepts of Montanus as absolute.

[9] De Labriolle, *op. cit.*, p. 64.

[10] Duchesne, *The Early History of the Church*, III, 548.

pagans and Jews; others refute the heretics of his age: the Valentinians, the Marcionites, and the Monarchians; many are pastoral and practical in character, dealing with penance, prayer, patience, second marriage, the theater, spectacles, idolatrous practices, feminine attire, and the wearing of the veil by young girls. Whether written in defense of Christian belief and discipline or against the practices of his former brethren, the character of his treatises is polemical.

Foremost among the writings of Tertullian is his remarkable work, the *Apologeticum*, which appeared at the end of the year 197. Early in the same year he brought out his first important apologetic work, *Ad nationes*, in two books which indicate the later developments in the *Apologeticum*. The former treatise was addressed to unbelievers in general, while the latter was intended for the benefit of all magistrates in whose hands practically rested the fate of the Christians. The introductory part of the *Apologeticum* presents judicial arguments against the laws of persecution. Tertullian then refutes the crimes alleged as being committed in Christian worship, after which he exposes the futility of pagan belief and practice, thereby exonerating the Christians from the charges of contempt of the state religion and high treason. The closing chapters of the work logically assert the supremacy of Christianity. The doctrines of the philosophers are discredited in the light of Christian doctrine because Christianity is a revealed religion.

There is a close resemblance between the *Octavius* of Minucius Felix [11] and the *Apologeticum* of Tertullian. It is generally conceded that one of these books must have been influenced by the other, but the question of which one enjoys priority is still a matter of disagreement among historians.[12]

Tertullian was evidently familiar with the apologetic writings of Justin Martyr, but a comparison of the *Apologeticum* with the *Apologies* of Justin reveals the superior literary talent and masterful logical ability of Tertullian. Whereas the *Apologies* of Justin lack an orderly arrangement and are conciliatory, the *Apologeticum* of Tertullian, with its irresistible logical power, demands for Christians the rights which unjust laws deprive them of and presents its ideas in such connected order that the whole work constitutes a methodically written and eloquent composition.[13]

Tertullian inaugurated Latin Christian literature in the West. Up to his time the Greek language was used in speculative Christian writing; he was the first

[11] Minucius was born in Africa in the second century. He probably became a lawyer in Rome and was afterward converted to Christianity. The *Octavius* shows that its author is a talented and refined writer seeking to disabuse the minds of men of culture of their prejudices toward Christianity. It is in the form of a dialogue and is in its way a work of art.

[12] De Labriolle, *op. cit.*, pp. 128–30.

[13] *Ibid.*, pp. 67–70.

creator of a Latin Christian diction to express thoughts and ideas unknown to the pagan writers.[14] The theology of the Western Christians is consequently indebted to him for much of its technical terminology.[15] Some of the most exact theological terms found in the Latin Church originated with him. In treating of moral problems in relation to the development of Catholic life in such heterogeneous surroundings as Carthage presented, he takes up the question of allowing Christians to share in pagan learning and to teach profane literature. He was not opposed to Christians' study of pagan literature, but he looked with disfavor upon their teaching it.[16] Despite his unsound reputation, his writings were abundantly used by his immediate successors and those of later centuries, so that the influence he has exercised as the first Latin interpreter of Christian thought in the West entitles him to recognition among the great masters.[17]

St. Cyprian

Thascius Caecilius Cyprianus (c. 200–258) regarded Tertullian as his master, and is said to have read a part of his works every day. Like Tertullian, he was born a pagan, received an excellent training

[14] Fowler, *A History of Roman Literature*, p. 247.
[15] Bardenhewer, *op. cit.*, p. 180.
[16] Hodgson, *Primitive Christian Education*, p. 193.
[17] Bardy, *op. cit.*, p. 36.

in rhetoric, and practiced law in the city of Carthage. The year of his birth is uncertain but it is generally believed to be about the beginning of the third century.[18] He became interested in the teachings of Christianity through contact with an aged priest, Caecilius, who converted him to the faith about 246 and whose name Cyprian added to his own. After distributing a part of his fortune among the poor, he became a priest, and at the end of the year 248 or at the beginning of 249 was chosen bishop of Carthage.[19]

During the next ten years Cyprian is the noble metropolitan of proconsular Africa. The persecutions under Decius and Valerian, the schism in his Church, the treatment of the lapsed, the validity of baptism conferred by heretics, and the defense of the unity of the Catholic Church and the role of the bishop in it constitute a series of crises in which he took part. Having through flight escaped death in the persecution under Decius, he fell a victim to the orders issued for the extirpation of the clergy under Valerian in 258. The year previous he had been sent into exile, but the second edict of Valerian marked him for death. Beheaded in his episcopal city on September 14, 258,[20] he was the first of the African bishops to suffer martyrdom. As a saint his name is

[18] Bardenhewer, *op. cit.*, p. 190.
[19] De Labriolle, *op. cit.*, p. 137.
[20] Bardy, *op. cit.*, p. 41.

equally revered in the Eastern and the Western Church.

The writings of Cyprian comprise treatises and letters. Of the eighty-one letters in the Cyprian collection, sixty-five are written by himself while the others are addressed to him. These letters are especially valuable for the information they give on early Church history. Of thirteen treatises his immortal work is the *De Catholicae Ecclesiae unitate*, which is a forceful declaration on the unity of the Catholic Church. This concept is the central theme running through all his writings and explains his attitude concerning the preponderant authority of the bishop.[21] The treatise bears witness to the fact that bishops are the guardians of the deposit of faith and the authorized arbiters of controversies, while the sovereignty of the bishop of Rome is based on Christ's address to St. Peter.[22] Because of certain statements in the *De unitate* which emphasize the unity of each particular Church of which the bishop is the head, rather than the unity of the universal Church, Anglican divines have frequently appealed to its authority to support their stand against the primacy of Rome.

The influence of Cyprian is evident from the almost countless manuscripts of his works and the large number of treatises which have been erroneously ascribed to him. The only Christian books

[21] De Labriolle, *op. cit.*, p. 139.
[22] Battifol, *Primitive Catholicism*, pp. 359–63.

which he seems to know are the Bible and the works of Tertullian. He never quotes pagan authors. His ability as a brilliant Latin writer is evident in proportion as his pastoral duties call forth his ideas. His qualities as a writer make of him a Christian classic.[23] Until the days of Jerome and Augustine his writings were unrivaled in the West. The reservations St. Augustine makes about baptism do not lessen his regard for Cyprian's works which had merited extraordinary popularity and almost universal respect.[24] His prestige as an author was recognized throughout the whole Christian world, and many of the images and allegories which color his compositions are found as commonplaces among later ecclesiastical writers.[25]

LACTANTIUS

Lucius Caelius Firmianus Lactantius (c. 250–? 330), a native of Africa, was born of pagan parents about 250.[26] According to St. Jerome, he studied under Arnobius [27] at Sicca and, like his master, be-

[23] Bardy, *op. cit.*, p. 45.
[24] De Labriolle, *op. cit.*, p. 162.
[25] Bardenhewer, *op. cit.*, p. 193.
[26] De Labriolle, *op. cit.*, p. 200.
[27] Arnobius was a famous rhetorician at Sicca-Veneria in proconsular Africa. He was suddenly converted to Christianity late in life. Because of his previous violent hatred of the Christian religion, the bishop of Sicca was a little skeptical of his conversion and demanded of him proof of his sincerity.

came a professor of rhetoric. His reputation as a rhetorician attracted the attention of Diocletian who appointed him a public teacher of Latin at Nicomedia, in Bithynia, which was made the new imperial city. It was difficult for Lactantius to arouse interest in Latin literature among pupils in this Greek town, so that he was forced to take to writing. He was converted to Christianity about the year 300.[28]

Diocletian's persecution did not force Lactantius to discontinue his career as a Christian teacher, but under Galerius he was obliged to leave Nicomedia until the edict of toleration was issued. Meanwhile he had suffered many privations and was reduced to penury. His subsequent life, however, was more peaceful. Through his friendship with Constantine he was called by the Emperor to be the tutor of his son, Crispus. This appointment took him later to Trier in Gaul when his young charge was sent to that city. He may have died there, but of the place and time of his death nothing is definitely known.[29]

The first three books of his *Divinae institutiones*

He wrote an apologetic work in seven books, *Adversus nationes*, in which he condemned pagan religions and vigorously defended Christianity. His apology reveals that he had little knowledge of the Christian religion. He had not yet received baptism, was unacquainted with most of the Bible, and knew nothing of the apologists who preceded him. His work showed by its style that the author was a trained rhetorician employing his education in the service of Christianity.

[28] Bardy, *op. cit.*, p. 59.
[29] Bardenhewer, *op. cit.*, p. 203.

are a critical evaluation of false religions and of ancient philosophy. The remaining four books are constructive in character, treating successively of the fundamental articles of the new faith, of the proper understanding of justice, of the immortality of the soul and the life of the blessed. Lactantius later made a revision of this treatise, called *Epitome divinarum institutionum* in which he summarizes his treatment of the subjects dealt with in the larger work, eliminating what he regarded as irrelevant and unsuited to the Christian conduct of life.

The *Divine Institutes* is not merely an apology, but a manual of theology as well. In fact, it is the first attempt by a Western writer to give a systematic exposition of Christian theology.[30] Despite its errors, which show the author's lack of accurate interpretation of the Scriptures and his acceptance of the so-called Sibylline oracles, it became a standard work for following generations. From the period of the Carlovingian revival of learning down to the Renaissance, numerous copies of this manuscript were made. The humanists echoed the praise given to Lactantius by St. Jerome, who regarded him as a model of Ciceronian elegance, designating him the Christian Cicero. St. Augustine, Cassiodorus, and St. Isidore recommended him highly. The great respect which these eminent educators manifested toward him prepared the way for the universal ad-

[30] *Ibid.*, p. 205.

miration which he won among men of culture and lent weight to the authority which he was to enjoy throughout the Middle Ages.[31]

THE GREAT DOCTORS

The fourth and fifth centuries are the age of the great Western Fathers. In this era Hilary, Ambrose, Jerome, and Augustine are the four commanding personalities. They surpassed all their Latin contemporaries and by their ecclesiastical leadership and knowledge were most potent in creating medieval thought.[32] With the Edict of Milan in the year 313 the fetters which had hampered the free action of the Church were broken and Christians were put on a social and political equality with pagans. The enemies of Catholic orthodoxy are no longer the pagans but the schismatics and heretics. The Donatist Schism was the chief anxiety of African Christianity while Arianism engaged the attention of the Church in Italy, Illyria, and Gaul. For the expansion of the spiritual power of the Church apologetical treatises were not demanded, but rather, doctrinal treatises, homilies, historical works, and a more faithful version of the Bible for the Christians of the West. The greatest Catholic Latin writer in the heroic struggle of the Church with the Arians and Emperor Constantius is St. Hilary of Poitiers.

[31] Rand, *Founders of The Middle Ages*, p. 63.
[32] Taylor, *The Classical Heritage of the Middle Ages*, p. 14.

St. Hilary of Poitiers

St. Hilary of Poitiers (c. 310–320—367), because of his defense of orthodoxy in the Western Church, is often called "the Athanasius of the West." He was born of one of the noble pagan families of Poitiers, probably between 310 and 320.[33] His early education was in keeping with the best traditions of the literary circles of Aquitania. After a study of the Scriptures, he gave up idleness and riches and was converted to Christianity. Shortly after his baptism he was chosen bishop of his native city. Because of his courageous attitude in defending the orthodox faith against the Arian influence which was spread throughout Gaul by the envoys of Emperor Constantius, five years of his episcopate were spent in exile. His banishment to Phrygia led him to appreciate deeply the speculative power displayed in the writings of the Fathers of the East and gave him a training in logic which fitted him for the leading role he was to play among the dialecticians of the West.[34]

So great was Hilary's activity among his Eastern colleagues that the Arians feared his influence and requested the Emperor to send him back to his see. In Gaul he witnessed the triumph of Nicene doctrine and from there carried the fight against Arian-

[33] Bardenhewer, *op. cit.*, p. 403.
[34] De Labriolle, *op. cit.*, p. 240.

ism into Italy. Emperor Valentinian, who protected the Arian bishop of Milan, ordered Hilary back to Poitiers, where he spent his last days writing exegetical treatises and historical works. He died in 367.[35]

The principal work of Hilary is his *De Trinitate*, a dogmatic treatise in twelve books written while in exile. The first book treats of the necessity of a true knowledge of God. The second explains the mystery of the Incarnation on the basis of the baptismal formula. The following six books defend the divinity of the Son, refute the objections against it, and prove that the doctrine of the sonship does not negate the unity of God. In books nine to eleven inclusive the author replies to the Arian arguments. The final book contains general remarks against Arianism and describes how the eternal birth of the Son is completely different from that of a temporal being. The *De synodis*, which has become an integral part of the *De Trinitate*, is a valuable treatise from the historical point of view. It acquaints the people of the West with the struggles in the East against Arianism and indicates that Hilary is at his best as a theologian setting forth the Nicene faith.

The importance of Hilary as a true teacher is seen from the fact that he has merited the distinction of being designated *Doctor of the Universal Church*. St. Augustine recognized him as an illustrious expounder of the Scriptures and an intrepid defender

[35] *Ibid.*, p. 250.

of the faith. St. Jerome, although severe in his criticism of Hilary's style, regarded his writings most favorably from the standpoint of Catholic teaching. His reputation as a master in doctrine did not diminish even when men appealed to Ambrose, Jerome, and Augustine as authorities.[36] As an intermediary between the theology of the East and that of the West, he gave to the latter many ideas of method and new expressions of thought. This influence is apparent in the subsequent development of Latin theology.[37]

St. Ambrose

Like Hilary, it was to the theological discourses of the Eastern Fathers that St. Ambrose (c. 340–397) turned for dogmatic and moral guidance in his struggle against the heterodoxy of the times. Through diligent study of the Bible and sympathetic reading of the Greek theologians he acquired the theological learning that enabled him as a bishop and an ecclesiastical statesman to employ his gifts of Roman genius in proclaiming a union between Church and state, one supreme in spiritual matters, the other in temporal. Although born of noble Christian parents at Trier, probably about 340,[38] Ambrose

[36] Duchesne, *op. cit.*, II, 416.
[37] Bardenhewer, *op. cit.*, p. 405. Cf. Grabmann, *op. cit.*, p. 120.
[38] *Ibid.*, p. 431.

lived his early life in Rome, where he was educated
in the liberal studies. His first ambition was to follow
in the footsteps of his father, who had been Praetorian Prefect of the Gauls. He began his career as a
lawyer. His eloquence won the esteem of Probus,
the Praetorian Prefect of Italy, who appointed him
consular governor of the provinces of Liguria and
Aemilia, with residence at Milan, the first city in the
West after Rome; there he ruled with firmness and
wisdom.[39]

In the violent disputes which arose among the
Christians of Milan, some of whom were partisans
of Arius, during the election of the new bishop of
the city, Ambrose entered the basilica to maintain
order; but the Milanese, recognizing in him the natural qualities of a great churchman as well as
of a great statesman, unanimously elected him their
bishop. The choice evidently appeared so excellent
to all that it was immediately approved by the Italian
bishops and Emperor Valentinian. When chosen
bishop, Ambrose was only a catechumen. According to the custom of those times his baptism had been
deferred; but he was now baptized and eight days
later was consecrated bishop, on the seventh of De-
cember, 374.[40]

The twenty-three years of Ambrose's episcopate

[39] Pierre de Labriolle, *The Life and Times of St. Ambrose.*
Translated from the French by Herbert Wilson (St. Louis:
B. Herder Company, 1928), p. v.
[40] Bardenhewer, *op. cit.,* p. 431.

were crowded with multifarious duties in the midst of which he was able to publish doctrinal and moral treatises, deliver numerous sermons, write many letters of a personal and official character, and compose hymns and poems. Most of his literary works deal chiefly with moral and practical subjects, the material of which was furnished by his catechetical instructions. After he delivered his sermons and homilies, the subject matter was put in written form and constituted a published treatise.[41]

The conduct of Ambrose in troubles he had to face from the very beginning of his episcopate revealed his talent for administration and made him conspicuous in maintaining the Christian cause. He forbade the restoration of the altar of Victory to its ancient place in the Hall of the Senate and repeatedly protested against any concession that promoted the practice of idolatry.[42] He showed himself firm and fearless in opposing the intrigues of Empress Justina who had surrounded herself with Arian Goths. When she instructed her son, Valentinian II, to request Ambrose to give up a basilica claimed by the Arians, he resolutely refused.[43] He reproved Theodosius for his decision in the affair of Callinicum, a chief town in Mesopotamia, where it was alleged that a Jewish synagogue had been burnt with

[41] De Labriolle, *op. cit.*, p. xi.
[42] *Ibid.*, pp. 3–39.
[43] *Ibid.*, pp. 39–56.

the complicity of ecclesiastical authority. He reproached the Emperor for having condemned the Bishop unheard and succeeded in having him amend his rescript.[44] For a second time he humbled Theodosius when he imposed a public penance on him after the massacre of Thessalonica. Because certain officials of the city were slain in a riot which had arisen from trivial causes, the Emperor determined upon reprisals and issued an order, following which the circus was invaded by soldiers who there massacred several thousand men, women, and children. Excluded from the Church by his cruel abuse of power, Theodosius gave evidence of sincere repentance in order to obtain reinstatement.[45] These instances of the religious policy of Ambrose indicate that in matters of faith and the moral law he declared and upheld the principle that bishops are judges of the Christian emperors, and not the emperors of the bishops.[46]

The Catholic loyalty which Gratian and Theodosius manifested toward Ambrose was due to his goodness and uprightness. He labored with them to make the Roman Empire a Christian empire in which there would be the absolute mutual dependence of Church and state with the Catholic faith the unifying force. He regarded the Roman Empire and

[44] Dudden, *The Life and Times of St. Ambrose*, pp. 372–78.
[45] *Ibid.*, pp. 381–91.
[46] *Ibid.*, pp. 500 f.

the Catholic Church as two aspects of the one society of which Rome seemed the predestined capital,
fulfilling a kind of providential mission in the diffusion of Christianity.[47] Five years after Ambrose'
death in 397, Alaric invaded Italy and later succeeded in taking Rome. A century after Ambrose'
death the Empire had fallen a prey to the invasions
of the barbarians. Four hundred years later the
ideal of Ambrose concerning the relation between
Church and state was to be re-created with the restoration of the imperial dignity under Charlemagne.

The principal work of Ambrose as a moralist is
his *De officiis ministrorum,* the plan of which is
based on the model of Cicero's *De officiis.* As Cicero
addressed his work to his son, so Ambrose in his
official position as a bishop writes to instruct his
spiritual sons, the clergy under his jurisdiction, since
grace impels to love just as strongly as nature. Cicero,
in writing his treatise for his son Marcus, pointing
out to him the proper conduct of the young gentle-
man, was at the same time interpreting philosophy
to the public. Ambrose undertook a similar service
of interpretation, intending his treatise to serve as a
manual of morality for all Christians. While Ambrose pays great tribute to Cicero in the order and
disposition of this famous work and as a Christian
humanist encourages the study of ancient literature,

[47] De Labriolle, *The Life and Times of St. Ambrose,* pp.
xviii f.

the plan of his argument is a challenge to Cicero and the whole pagan scheme of decent conduct. The purpose of his treatise is not to reconcile pagan culture with Christian truth but to demonstrate that the Sacred Scriptures and the lives of Christians illustrate abundantly the excellent precepts which are found in the pagan ethical structure. The difference between the Christian and the pagan point of view concerning the scale of duties lies in the emphasis on the spiritual truth proclaimed in Christian moral doctrine that the duty toward God must head the list.[48]

The three books of the *De officiis ministrorum* [49] treat of the good and the useful in relation to eternal life. Cicero distinguished between the *bonum* and the *utile* in his treatment of *officia*. Ambrose denies this distinction, contending that everything good must be useful and that the utility of a thing should be reckoned not from the viewpoint of the world only but from its usefulness for eternity. He likewise denies that what is becoming is a secondary virtue. Everything good is becoming, and nothing is good unless it is becoming. Goodness is the substance, what is becoming is the form. Further he speaks in the first book of the duties to be observed throughout life and discusses the cardinal virtues of wisdom, moderation, justice, and bravery.

[48] Rand, *op. cit.*, pp. 80 f.
[49] Migne, *Patr. lat.*, XVI, 18–184.

The second book considers what constitutes ulti-
mate happiness. Eternal life is the fruit of virtue.
The riches of this world are a hindrance to the attainment of that blessedness. Utility lies not in making money, but in gaining piety. What is useful is
also just. It is just that we serve Christ who has re-
deemed us.

The third book continues this practical discussion
of the details of right Christian conduct. It points out
that there is no conflict between the good and the
useful since nothing can be morally good that is not
useful, and nothing useful that is not morally good.
In this respect the author agrees with Cicero. In
other instances throughout the treatise he favors the
Stoics, but in setting forth his rules of Christian
morality it is always Christianity that forms the decisive element.

St. Ambrose' *De officiis* is the first noteworthy
synthesis of the Western Church dealing with moral
problems.[50] It is a new sort of apology, seeking to
state simple formulas derived from a study of the
Scriptures. Because of its practical purpose in relation to the religious and moral life of man, it became
a mirror of conduct for succeeding generations and
was of influence throughout the Middle Ages. Although Ambrose followed Cicero very closely in
the arrangement of his ideas and in his expressions,
the merit of the treatise lies in the ability of its author

[50] De Labriolle, *op. cit.*, p. 277.

to translate the system of Cicero into contemporary terms.[51]

Ambrose was content for the most part to adapt the thoughts of others to the circumstances of his times. He often reproduces the ideas of an earlier Christian or pagan writer in an effort to gather a second crop of thought from a field already worked.[52] His writings, which comprise every class of theological literature, make no claim to greatness in either scholarship or theology, yet they stamp him as a completely Christian Roman destined to be regarded by succeeding ages as the great father of medieval Christianity.[53] He gave a powerful impetus to the monastic movement in the West, contributed to the poetry and music of the Church, promoted the veneration of the saints and their relics, and shaped much of the thought of the Middle Ages by his teaching on theology and Christian ethics.[54]

St. Jerome

St. Jerome (c. 331 or 340–420) was born about the same time as St. Ambrose. While Ambrose was ruling in the episcopal chair of Milan as a distinguished bishop, Jerome was living a monastic life in Bethlehem, putting his remarkable scholarship at the

[51] Rand, *op. cit.*, p. 82.
[52] Bardenhewer, *op. cit.*, p. 435.
[53] Taylor, *op. cit.*, p. 78.
[54] Dudden, *op. cit.*, p. 496.

service of Christianity and launching a current of thought that was to dominate the Western Church for the next thousand years. Jerome is the great Christian scholar of his age.[55] He was born in the city of Stridon on the confines of Dalmatia and Pannonia, in Illyria, about 331 in the opinion of some authorities, and not before 340 [56] according to others. His parents were well-to-do Christians, but Jerome was not baptized until he was a young man, despite the fact that theologians at that time strove to discredit the practice of putting off baptism. He had come to Rome to complete his education and, after a somewhat dissipated life, repented of his misconduct and was baptized there. His teacher at Rome was the celebrated pagan grammarian, Donatus, who instructed him in the Latin classics, particularly Terence and Vergil. No other Christian writer except St. Augustine was so well nurtured on the pith of the classics.[57]

In the years that followed until 382, Jerome is to be found successively in Gaul; in the city of Trier, one of the great seats of culture in the fourth century, where he is interested in theology largely through the reading of the works of St. Hilary; at Aquileia, where he is associated in the practice of asceticism with a group of friends among them

[55] Sandys, *A History of Classical Scholarship*, I, 232.

[56] Bardenhewer, *op. cit.*, p. 455.

[57] De Labriolle, *History and Literature of Christianity*, p. 336.

Rufinus, with whom he later engaged in bitter controversy on Origenism; in the East, in Syria, where he fell ill of a fever and had his famous dream in which he was rebuked for his excessive fondness for reading the classics; in the desert of Chalcis, where he led a hermit's life for five years, engaging in manual work, the transcription of manuscripts, and the study of Hebrew; revisiting Antioch, where he was ordained a priest with exemption from pastoral cares. In 380 he settled at Constantinople. There he studied under Gregory of Nazianzus, meanwhile completing his study of Greek. Two years later he returned to Rome; there Pope Damasus welcomed him as a scholar and counsellor and turned his attention to the study of the Scriptures.

At the instance of the Pope, Jerome began a revision and translation of the Bible. This work made demands upon his scholarly attainments during the next twenty years of his life. Because of the favor in which he was held by Damasus, he was spoken of as his successor. But on the death of the Pontiff, the opposition he had incurred during his three years as secretary to the Roman See caused him to leave Rome and retire to the East. His unpopularity was owing to protests against corrections in his revision of the Gospels, his encouragement of ascetical propaganda, and the influence he had gained in high society over the Christian ladies of Rome.[58]

[58] Duchesne, *op. cit.*, II, 381.

After departing for the East, Jerome settled at Bethlehem. Here he was joined by the saintly Paula and her daughter, Eustochium. Paula employed what she had left of her fortune to build a monastery over which Jerome presided and several convents which she administered herself. Jerome now spent the happiest period of his life lecturing on the Scriptures to his monks and teaching grammar and the classical authors in the school for boys which he had opened in connection with the monastery. The happiness of this period was marred by the quarrels over Origenism in which his former friend, Rufinus, became his avowed enemy. Rufinus attributed to Jerome his own efforts in favor of Origen. Thereupon Jerome, with his sarcastic and humanistic pen, vented his feelings on his adversary. Jerome protested that, although Rufinus and he had studied Origen together in their youth, he admired Origen not for his faith but for his genius as a scholar.[59]

The declining years of Jerome's life witnessed the decease of many of his pious and learned friends, the sack of his monastery by fanatical Pelagians, the taking of Rome by the Goths, and the barbarian invasion of Palestine. After a long and fruitful life consecrated to the service of God and the Church, this profoundly human saint of an impulsive though disciplined temperament, weary with the weight of years and the burdens of cares and sorrows, died in

[59] De Labriolle, *op. cit.*, p. 372.

his cell at Bethlehem on the thirtieth of September, 420.[60]

In the calm atmosphere of Bethlehem, Jerome carried out his program of scholarship which merits for him a place of distinction among the leading scholars and humanists of all times. It was during his retirement in the East that he wrote the lives of three hermits of the desert, Paul, Malchus, and Hilarion. With these small masterpieces he gave a new character to hagiographic literature and initiated a line of tradition that endured throughout the Middle Ages, culminating in the Golden Legend of Jacopo de Voragine.[61] That he might have done excellent work as a historian is shown from his translation, revision, and continuation of the *Chronicle* of Eusebius dictated at Constantinople. This work contributed to the Middle Ages the history of empires and became one of the fundamental books in the work of research on the past of mankind.[62] His *De viris illustribus*, in imitation of treatises of Suetonius, is another indication of his interest in the past. It is the earliest manual of patristics, in which one hundred and thirty-five known and otherwise unknown Christian writers are treated. Jerome does not hesitate to include the names of heretics, because he

[60] Bardenhewer, *op. cit.*, p. 459.
[61] Rand, *op. cit.*, p. 121.
[62] De Labriolle, *op. cit.*, p. 344.

feels that they have made a contribution to Christian thinking. Despite evidences the work contains of his sympathies and antipathies which are not proper to the historian and critic, this valuable literary history inspired later writers, such as Gennadius, St. Isidore of Seville, and Honorius of Autun, to continue the purpose and plan of the work.[63]

The monumental work of Jerome's life was his preparation of a Latin text of the Bible from the Greek and Hebrew versions. While he was in Rome, at the request of Pope Damasus he revised the old Latin version used at that time, called the *Itala*. When this rendering was completed it included the whole New Testament and the Psalms. The new Latin text of the Psalter, called the *Psalterium Romanum*, was used in Rome until the latter part of the sixteenth century.[64] Parts of it are still found in the Roman breviary. In Bethlehem, Jerome studied the *Hexapla*, or sixfold text of Origen, and began a new revision of the Old Testament based not merely on the Greek versions but also on the Hebrew text. Only the Psalms have survived in this version, which is known as the *Psalterium Gallicanum* because it was current in Gaul; it has remained in use in the Church to this day. Finally, Jerome turned from the work of revising old translations to a direct translation of the

[63] *Ibid.*, p. 364.
[64] Laistner, *op. cit.*, p. 46.

Old Testament from such Hebrew and Aramaic manuscripts as were accessible to him. To this new translation was added the Gallican Psalter and the New Testament revised from the venerated *Vetus Latina*.[65] This third version, under the title of the *Vulgate*, indicating its common use, was officially adopted by the Council of Trent. Jerome's knowledge of Latin, Greek, and Hebrew, together with his profitable experimentation in the study of the Bible, served to make the *Vulgate*, taken as a whole, a model of elegant and exact translation.[66] He rendered a vast service to the Church by giving to the Christian world the Word of God in a unified and fixed text. In the Middle Ages the existence of his successive versions of the Psalter stimulated an interest in textual criticism.[67]

St. Jerome was a born teacher. Scattered throughout his numerous letters are many ideas of practical educational value, but in two letters particularly he deals professedly with the subject of education. These letters were the guides for the education of girls throughout the Middle Ages. One is a letter written at Bethlehem to Laeta [68] at Rome in 403 on

[65] Martin Schanz, *Geschichte der römischen Literatur* (München: C. H. Beck'sche Verlagsbuchhandlung, 1914), 2nd ed., IV, 1, 451–56.

[66] Laistner, *op. cit.*, p. 47.

[67] Sandys, *op. cit.*, p. 234.

[68] *Epist.* 107; Migne, *Patr. lat.*, XXII, 867–78; *Select Library of Nicene and Post-Nicene Fathers*, 2nd ser., VI, 189–95.

the education of her daughter Paula. The second is a shorter letter to Gaudentius,[69] a Roman, on the education of his daughter Pacatula. It was written from Bethlehem in 413. These parents, in accordance with a religious custom of the day, had consecrated their daughters to a life of virginity and had written to Jerome for advice on how to rear their children. They were to live apart from the world and eventually to become nuns in convents. It is apparent that the training outlined in both letters is the ideal training of the girl who is not to live an ordinary life in the world. Jerome realized, however, that the principles he was about to lay down were equally applicable to any child. These principles are universally sound and can be as profitably applied today as they were in his time.

According to Jerome, the process of education should unfold the latent mental and spiritual abilities of the child with the purpose of developing a virtuous and moral character. Early education should be a training of the natural powers for the advantageous reception of supernatural truth. In regard to the early training of children, his ideas reflect the opinions of Quintilian, the distinguished Roman pagan educator of the first century. Jerome ardently admired the writings of Quintilian, but he was quite aware that the virility of the old Roman stock which

[69] *Epist.* 128, Migne, XXII, 1095-99; *Nicene and Post-Nicene Fathers*, VI, 258-60.

Quintilian represented had largely disappeared in his time. The turbulent fourth century was characterized by the decay of patriotism and a general dissoluteness on the part of the people. Jerome was determined to counteract the vain and sensuous education of the day and especially to oppose the degrading practices of the pagan world in matters of sex. Many of his ideas may seem extreme to the modern educator, but viewed in the light of the period in which they were advanced they will not appear so radical.

The soundness of most of his educational principles and his insight into child psychology may be gleaned from his observations regarding the early stage of education.

And let her have companions in her lessons to excite emulation in her, that she may be stimulated when she sees them praised. You must not scold her if she is slow to learn, but must employ praise to excite her mind, so that she may be glad when she excels others or sorry when she is excelled by them. Above all, you must take care not to make her lessons distasteful to her lest a dislike for them conceived in childhood may continue into her mature years. The very words which she tries bit by bit to put together and to pronounce ought not to be chance ones, but names especially fixed upon and heaped together for the purpose, those for example of the prophets or the apostles or the list of patriarchs from Adam downwards as it is given by Matthew and Luke. In this way while her tongue will be well-trained, her memory will be likewise developed.

Again you must choose for her a master of approved years, life, and learning. A man of culture will not, I think, blush to do for a kinswoman or a high-born virgin what Aristotle did for Philip's son when, descending to the level of an usher, he consented to teach him his letters. Things must not be despised as of small account in the absence of which great results cannot be achieved. The very rudiments and first beginnings of knowledge sound differently in the mouth of an educated man or of an uneducated.[70]

Jerome showed great concern for careful parental direction, maintaining that the real beginnings of Christian education are made in the home. He outlined for the girl a program of mental development consisting of reading, writing, spelling, syntax, Latin and Greek; [71] advocated instruction in the manual arts befitting her sex; and insisted on the spiritual aim of all learning. Education could attain to its highest perfection only when accompanied by moral excellence. Learning was to nurture the soul in righteousness and develop a cheerful spirituality. The greatest intellectual joy was to be gotten from the study of Holy Scriptures which, if rightly taught, would produce the ideal Christian. The way of acquiring virtue was to be learned from the Sacred Writings.

[70] *Epist.* 107; Migne, XXII, *op. cit.*, 871 f.; *Nicene and Post-Nicene Fathers*, VI, 191.
[71] The grandmother, Paula, and the aunts, Blesilla and Eustochium, of little Paula knew Hebrew and studied the Scriptures and sang the psalms in the language in which they had been written.

They were to be the sole interest of the young girl destined for convent life. She was to find in them her delight, her consolation, and her joy.[72]

Jerome encouraged emulation in the training of children as an important incentive to effort. He discouraged the parrot fashion method of learning, insisting that the words Paula uses must have a natural connection so that her memory may be trained and strengthened by a process of association. He wishes Laeta to choose for Paula "a master of approved years, life, and learning," arguing that the first beginnings of knowledge should be imparted by an educated and cultured teacher.

Concerning physical education, Jerome favored plain food. He deprecates "long and immoderate fasts" for the young, maintaining that a child of tender years should not fast; then, again, an overstrained ideal is often responsible for despair. He prohibited bathing on the part of full-grown girls; but allowed the use of the bath to children. In this matter he was not so much opposed to cleanliness, but to the public baths where women were more or less exposed to moral ruin.

The letters of Jerome on the subject of the education of girls were widely quoted throughout the Middle Ages. His scholarship and humanism were

[72] William H. Russell, *St. Jerome as an Educator* (unpublished Master's thesis, The Catholic University of America, 1921), pp. 20 f.

universally recognized by medieval teachers. The
estimate made of him by Cassiodorus in his *Di-*
vinae institutiones ratified the favorable judgment of
Jerome's contemporaries, such as Augustine, Sulpi-
cius Severus, and Cassian, and determined the opinion of him that was to be held by the Schoolmen of
the Middle Ages. The Scholastics drew inspiration
and guidance not only from his prefaces to the books
of the Bible, but from his numerous commentaries
and controversial works.[73] His letter to Paulinus on
the study of the Bible was prefixed to each of the
many copies of Alcuin's version of the text.[74] Jerome's extensive correspondence, which comprises
about a hundred and twenty-five letters dealing with
a variety of subjects, reveals that men and women of
all social ranks wrote to him and were answered by
him.[75] The language and style of his letters stamp
him as a great mediator between classical antiquity
and the times that came after him.[76] By his gifts as
a master of Latin prose, he was destined to exercise
a great influence upon the literature of the Middle
Ages in the West.[77] And at the same time, by his
zeal for the ascetic ideal he urged the practice of
fruitful celibacy devoted to good works, thereby
preparing the way for the expansion of Western

[73] Rand, *op. cit.*, p. 131.
[74] *Ibid.*, p. 132.
[75] Bardy, *op. cit.*, p. 109.
[76] Taylor, *op. cit.*, p. 212.
[77] De Labriolle, *op. cit.*, p. 373.

monasticism.[78] His ideas circulated in the Middle
Ages through his influential admirers, Lupus Serva-
tus, Hincmar, Honorius of Autun, and St. Bernard.
So highly did the humanist, John of Salisbury, regard his gifts as a man of letters and as a scholar that
he called him *doctorum doctissimus*.[79] This praise
was matched later by Erasmus, who compared his
style with that of Cicero,[80] proclaimed him the chief
of theologians,[81] and designated him as a man "*quo
vero nihil habet orbis Latinus vel doctius vel sanc-
tius*." [82]

St. Augustine

Jerome's distinguished contemporary, Augustine
(354–430)—Aurelius Augustinus—was not the
scholar and master of style that St. Jerome was, but
he was a greater thinker, in fact, one of the deepest
and most original thinkers of all time. In his discrimi-
nating estimate of the two, the humanist, Filelfo,
proposed that, were it possible to have made one in-
tellect from the two, then the force of nature could
have produced nothing greater.[83]

[78] *Ibid.*
[79] Rand, *op. cit.*, p. 132.
[80] *Opus epistolarum Des. Erasmi Roterodami denuo re-
cognitum et auctum per Percy S. Allen* (Oxford, Clarendon
Press, 1906), I, 332.
[81] *Loc. cit.*
[82] *Epist.* 613, *Des. Erasmi,* Leyden edition, 1703, Tomi Tertii
Pars Prior, 691 A.
[83] Rand, *op. cit.*, p. 251.

Augustine was born on November 13, 354, at Tagaste, a small town in Numidia.[84] His father was a pagan, but his mother, St. Monica, was a devout Christian. Although Monica gave his early education her individual attention, she did not have him baptized. Sent to Madaura, a nearby village, to continue his studies, Augustine developed a fondness for Latin and a distaste for Greek. He went to Carthage to finish his education. There he perfected himself in rhetoric, law, philosophy, and in every other science taught at this seat of learning. Meanwhile he formed an illicit union with the woman who bore his son, Adeodatus, and to her he remained faithful as if she were his wife.[85]

The success that Augustine attained as an orator at Carthage prompted him to make a deeper study of pagan philosophy. Having taken Cicero as his model, he read his dialogue *Hortensius*. In this treatise, Cicero, to whom he attributed the gift of prophecy, failed to mention the name of Christ.[86] From that time on Augustine longed to know the whole truth. He then turned to study the Scriptures, but he was dissatisfied with their simple style. He next joined the sect of the Manichaeans who, like the Gnostic sects, had absorbed some of the Christian teaching and had imitated Christian institutions. He

[84] Bardenhewer, *op. cit.*, p. 473.
[85] De Labriolle, *op. cit.*, p. 396.
[86] *Confessions;* Migne, *Patr. lat.*, XXXII, 686; *Select Library of the Nicene and Post-Nicene Fathers*, 1st ser., I, 62.

remained attached to that body for about nine years. Meanwhile he taught grammar at Tagaste and directed a school of rhetoric at Carthage. It was during this sojourn in Carthage that he appealed to the Manichaean bishop named Faustus to solve his doubts about certain points of doctrine. The evasive answers of the bishop led him to sever his connections with the sect.

Augustine now decided to go to Rome where, he had been told, the students were better disciplined and there was opportunity for higher appointment.[87] The students here proved to have little regard for honor, avoiding the payment of fees by enrolling in the school of another master when the tuition charges were due.[88] Disgusted with such conditions, Augustine gladly accepted an official professorship at Milan. As a master of rhetoric, he was drawn to attending the sermons of St. Ambrose, bishop of that city. The teachings of St. Ambrose gave him new intellectual appreciation and ultimately led to his definite conversion.

For a short time Augustine leaned toward the opinion of the academician philosophers who with their pessimistic skepticism maintained that man could not attain to the full understanding of any truth. Certain treatises of the Neoplatonists which

[87] De Labriolle, *op. cit.*, p. 399.
[88] *Confessions;* Migne, *Patr. lat.*, XXXII, 716; *Nicene and Post-Nicene Fathers,* 1st ser., I, 62.

had come into his hands convinced him that he could not long remain a skeptic. His reading of these Platonist books settled many metaphysical problems that had perplexed him and revealed to him a solution of the problem of evil.[89]

Eleven years had now passed since he set out at the age of nineteen to possess truth in its integrity. He had broken definitely with Manichaeism. He was beginning to understand certain Catholic doctrines which he had regarded as untenable and he had developed a favorable attitude toward the study of the Holy Scriptures. He gave up his teaching and decided to prepare for baptism. He withdrew the service of his tongue from the talk market, that boys "who thought not on Thy law, nor on Thy peace, but on mendacious follies and forensic strifes," might no longer purchase at his mouth equipment for their fury.[90]

In the autumn of 386 he retired to Cassiciacum, near Milan, accompanied by his mother and his son together with a brother and some friends. Here he led the pious little group in philosophic discussions and after eight months of meditation and prayer received baptism from the hands of St. Ambrose in the basilica of Milan.

Not long after his baptism Augustine decided to

[89] Bardy, *op. cit.*, p. 132.
[90] *Confessions;* Migne, *Patr. lat.*, XXXII, 763; *Nicene and Post-Nicene Fathers*, I, 129.

return to Africa. On the way there, at Ostia, his mother died, thus ending that beautiful relation which is one of the most moving features of his *Confessions*. Forced to spend several months in Rome, he afterward embarked for Carthage, visiting the scenes of his former educational activity, and finally settling in his native town. For three years he and his friends lived in a sort of monastery at Tagaste, their studious retreat saddened only by the early death of Adeodatus.

In his thirty-seventh year Augustine was ordained to the priesthood. He had made a journey to Hippo where the choice of the people designated him for the office when Valerius, the aged bishop of the city, made known to them the necessity of ordaining a new priest.[91] In a house and garden near the church, made over to him by the bishop, Augustine continued his monastic life. From this monastery developed other branches, one of which became an episcopal school and seminary.[92] Three years after his ordination Augustine, at the request of Valerius, was consecrated his coadjutor by Megalius,[93] primate of Numidia, and upon the death of the Bishop of Hippo he became his successor.

After his elevation to the episcopacy, Augustine

[91] Herbert T. Weiskotten, *Sancti Augustini vita scripta a Possidio Episcopo*. Edited with revised text and an English version (Princeton: Princeton University Press, 1909), p. 47.
[92] Newman, *Historical Sketches*, II, 161.
[93] Weiskotten, *op. cit.*, p. 57.

left the seclusion of his monastery, but he formed a religious community of priests, deacons, and subdeacons in the episcopal house. As bishop of Hippo he continued to live a monastic life with the clerics of his household.

During the nearly thirty-five years that he governed the Church of Africa his labors were remarkable for their extent and variety. Correspondents in Gaul, Italy, and Spain questioned him. He neglected no detail in order to assure the triumph of truth. As a polemist, he regarded his adversaries as brethren. Manichaeans, Donatists, Pelagians, and Arians recognized his remarkable powers of argumentation. His controversy with the Manichaeans revealed his ability as a commentator on Scripture; his struggle with the Donatists defined his position regarding the Church; his long conflict with the Pelagians won for him ecclesiastical approbation, both conciliar and pontifical, in matters of divine grace, its nature, necessity, and gratuitous character.

During the last years of his life, Augustine witnessed the rapid disintegration of the Roman Empire. The Vandals had overrun Africa and in time laid waste the land, sparing neither church nor private property. Fortunately Augustine was spared witnessing the devastation of Hippo. For three months he sustained the hopes of his people after the city had been besieged in May 430, but soon afterward he fell sick of fever and died the twenty-eighth of the following August at the age of seventy-six.[94]

Augustine stands unsurpassed among the Latin Fathers for the number of his works and the variety of the subjects treated. With the exception of Chrysostom, none of the Greek Fathers have contributed so much to ecclesiastical literature.[95] The best complete edition of his works is the Benedictine (Paris, 1679–1700), reprinted in Migne's *Patrologia* (XXXII–XLVII). His works include philosophical, apologetic, dogmatic, dogmatico-polemical, and exegetical writings, treatises of moral and practical theology, sermons, letters, and poems. All his writings are of an educational character if we consider education in its broad sense, but there are some that have more educational value than others. The *Confessions* is the work by which he is best known in general literature. It is one of the great books of all ages and is widely esteemed not only by students, but also by general readers.[96] Written about 400, a short time after Augustine's elevation to the episcopacy, it is a record of the great turning points in his progress from a Carthaginian sybarite to a Christian saint.

The *De Trinitate*, in fifteen books, the longest and most important of his dogmatic works, was be-

[94] Bardenhewer, *op. cit.,* p. 477.
[95] *Ibid.,* p. 494.
[96] In the small Oxford edition it is sold for a shilling. Cf. Leigh-Bennett, *Handbook of the Early Christian Fathers* (London: Williams and Norgate, 1920), p. 308.

gun about 410 and finished after 416.[97] It was written against the Arians who, although they had never made great progress in Africa, were sufficiently menacing to need refuting. In the first seven books of this treatise Augustine develops and proves the traditional teaching concerning the Trinity, and in the remaining eight he undertakes to defend the doctrine by showing how the human mind furnishes numerous analogies to it. Throughout the defense of his theses he is deeply conscious of the inability of philosophy to prove the truth and necessity of this mystery. He is content with setting forth in a reasoned system his mature faith in the Catholic doctrine.

The *De Civitate Dei*, in twenty-one books, was composed between 413 and 426.[98] The occasion of the work was the sack of Rome by Alaric and the Goths, and it was intended to disprove the false charge that the catastrophe was due to the abandonment of the ancient gods and the acceptance of Christianity. Begun with apologetic and polemical purpose, this treatise developed, as the author's horizon widened, into a masterly synthesis of the Christian philosophy of history.[99] The *Retractations* written toward the end of his life, when he was seventy-two years old,[100] consists of two books. In

[97] Bardenhewer, *op. cit.*, p. 481.
[98] *Ibid.*, p. 479.
[99] Bardy, *op. cit.*, p. 144.
[100] Bardenhewer, *op. cit.*, p. 477.

this work Augustine reviews the ninety-three treatises which he had written as layman, priest, and
bishop. He disavows his former regard for the philosophy of Plato, rejects certain Christian authors,
such as Origen, because of their insufficient orthodoxy, amends some of his biblical interpretations, and
modifies certain of his statements in doctrine.[101]

Meanwhile Augustine completed in 426 his *De
doctrina Christiana,* which he had begun almost
thirty years before. This, the most important of his
exegetical writings,[102] is divided into two parts. The
three books of the first part are a veritable manual of
hermeneutics; in the fourth book, or second part,
the intellectual formation of the Christian teacher is
outlined. Of Augustine's shorter treatises, the *De
catechizandis rudibus* is the only study dealing with
catechetical instruction for the *accedentes,* or candidates for admission to the catechumenate, that has
come down to us. It was composed about 400 and
was addressed to a deacon of Carthage, Deogratias,
who had asked Augustine for advice on the subject
matter and the method of catechists. The treatise is
unique because it is at once a manual for the catechist
and for the catechumen.[103] His *De magistro* which
was written in Africa, probably during the third

101 De Labriolle, *op. cit.,* p. 394.
102 Bardenhewer, *op. cit.,* p. 488.
108 Joseph P. Christopher, *Augustinus De catechizandis
rudibus* (Washington: The Catholic University of America,
1926), pp. 2 f.

year after his conversion, may be regarded as his farewell to philosophy.[104] Like all his philosophical works, it bears the marks of the Platonic and Ciceronian method of deduction. The work itself is a study of the nature and structure of language and the philosophy of teaching, and consequently of the philosophy of the learning process. Augustine also produced treatises that are *ex professo* educational. He wrote *De grammatica* and a portion of *De musica*, outlined the basic concepts of five other sections of the seven liberal arts, and drew up the principles of dialectics and rhetoric. These treatises were intended to form a great encyclopedia similar to that of Varro, but the work was never finished.[105]

The chief pedagogical ideas of Augustine are found in the *Confessions*. While in the mind of the author they are a hymn of praise and thanksgiving to God, they set forth at the same time a complete psychology of the human soul. The whole development of Augustine's mind may be traced in them. They show step by step his progress from childhood to mature manhood and, from his own life and experiences, portray the whole nature of man. In this work Augustine indicates how a word or a look may lead to evil inclination or stimulate to noble deed; emphasizes the importance of the senses in the acquisition of knowledge; analyzes the nature and

[104] Bardy, *op. cit.*, p. 138.
[105] Sandys, *op. cit.*, p. 236.

power of memory; treats of learning and thinking; and maintains that all teaching is based on faith and authority.[106] His philosophical point of view is the keynote of the entire work: "Thou hast formed us for Thyself, and our hearts are restless till they find rest in Thee." [107] The first nine books prove the truth of this principle from his personal experience. The tenth book, written at a later date, gives an account of what he then was. The last six chapters of this book are an ethical treatment of the three types of temptation corresponding in their order as given by St. John, to "the lust of the flesh, the lust of the eyes, and the pride of life." The remaining three books are a commentary on the creation narrative in Genesis. They are devoted to speculative philosophy, presenting in a remarkable devotional manner metaphysical treatises on the possibility of knowing God and the nature of time and space. The theology of the *Confessions* has entered into the very life blood of Western Christendom.

The *De Civitate Dei* [108] is considered the greatest of all Augustine's works.[109] The first ten books contain, as has been said, a refutation of the pagans' accusation that the travail of the Roman world was owing to the advent of Christianity. The last twelve, di-

---

[106] *Confessions;* Migne, *Patr. lat.,* XXXII, 779-95. *Nicene and Post-Nicene Fathers,* I, 142-52.

[107] Migne, *ibid.,* 661; *Nicene and Post-Nicene Fathers,* I, 45.

[108] Migne, *Patr. lat.,* XLI, 13-804.

[109] Bardy, *op. cit.,* p. 144. Cf. Bardenhewer, *op. cit.,* p. 479.

vided into groups of four, are a constructive exposition of the true nature and history of the city of God and the city of the world in which the course of human history from the fall of Adam through successive ages of time is regarded as part of an unending progress. Augustine's two cities are not Church and state. They have really no counterpart in the world as it exists, but belong to the period of final and decisive separation which will come when the end of the world takes place.

The city of God we speak of is the same to which testimony is borne by that Scripture, which excels all the writings of all nations by its divine authority, and has brought under its influence all kinds of minds, and this not by a casual intellectual movement but obviously by an express providential arrangement. For there it is written, "Glorious things are spoken of thee, O city of God." And in another psalm we read, "Great is the Lord, and greatly to be praised in the city of our God, in the mountain of His holiness, increasing the joy of the whole earth.". . . From these and similar testimonies, all of which were tedious to cite, we have learned that there is a city of God, and its Founder has inspired us with a love which makes us covet its citizenship. To this Founder of the holy city the citizens of the earthly city prefer their own gods, not knowing that He is the God of gods, not of false, i.e., of impious and proud gods, who being deprived of His unchangeable and freely communicated light, and so reduced to a kind of poverty-stricken power, eagerly grasp at their own private privilege, and seek divine honors from their deluded subjects; but of the pious and holy gods, who are better pleased to submit themselves to one, than to subject many to themselves, and who would rather worship God than be worshipped as God.[110]

The rewards of the celestial city, reserved for those who are good, are placed in happy contrast to the punishments of the earthly city, destined for those who are wicked.

And by another prophet he uttered the same prediction: "At that time thy people shall be delivered, every one that shall be found written in the book. And many of them that sleep in the dust" (or, as some interpret it, "in the mound") "of the earth shall awake, some to everlasting life, and some to shame and everlasting contempt." [111]

For Augustine, however, the earthly manifestation of the eternal city is the visible hierarchical Church, its organ and representative, which elevates the hopes of the Christian above the distresses of earthly misfortunes, creates in him a profound respect for his supernatural destiny, and guides him in his passage from time to eternity.

The occasion of the *De Civitate Dei* was an urgent need confronting Christianity after the occupation of Rome by the barbarians at the beginning of the fifth century. Yet it has remained, since it was written, a book for all time. Its appeal is as strong today as it was at the time of its writing fifteen hundred

[110] Quoted from xi, 1; *Nicene and Post-Nicene Fathers*, II, 205.

[111] Quoted from xxii, 3; *Nicene and Post-Nicene Fathers*, II, 481.

years ago. The same question, "Why does God allow it?" that was asked by the fugitives before the army of Alaric and the Goths is asked by fugitives before other invading armies. Augustine's answer evolved the Christian philosophy of history. History to him is the vast interval between the foundation of the universe and the last judgment, in which the terrestrial story of man must be interpreted in terms of the eternal will of God.[112]

The *De Civitate Dei* was widely read during the Middle Ages.[113] By means of it Augustine helped to transform the Roman Empire into the Holy Roman Empire. Einhart says that Emperor Charlemagne was especially fond of having this work read to him. Frequent references to it are found in the *Summa theologica* of Thomas Aquinas and in the *Polycraticus* of John of Salisbury.[114] The writings of Geraldus Cambrensis are indebted to it; the *Chronicon* of Otto of Freising adheres to Augustine's conception of the two cities in the *De Civitate Dei*.[115]

[112] Joseph P. Christopher, *St. Augustine: Founder of the Christian Philosophy of History* (Washington: the Catholic University of America, 1931), pp. 8–14.

[113] Grabmann, *Die Geschichte der Scholastischen Methode*, p. 136.

[114] J. E. C. Welldon, *St. Augustine De Civitate Dei* (New York: Macmillan Company, 1924), I, lii.

[115] In later times it was the inspiration of books that have dealt with the reformation of society. It has been a prolific source for Dante's *De monarchia*, for Bacon's *New Atlantis*, for More's *Utopia*, for Vico's *Scienza nuova*, for Grotius' *De jure belli ac pacis*, and for Leibnitz' *De jure suprematus*. Bos-

The views of Augustine on the right use of the various sciences, especially rhetoric, philosophy, and pagan literature, may be found in the *De doctrina Christiana*.[116] God is the author of all the arts and sciences. Therefore no knowledge that may be of service in the study of the divine sciences is to be discredited, not even that derived from pagan sources. History, natural history, astronomy, dialectics, rhetoric, and kindred subjects are worthy of study and should prove potent auxiliaries of exegesis and preaching. In the expression of truth, the Christian is free to use the natural sciences, but he must avoid the folly of the pagan who used these branches of learning as instruments of superstition. It is one thing to say that the juice of this herb will remove the pain in the stomach, and another to say that the cure can be effected by hanging the herb around the neck.[117]

The teachings of the pagan philosophers contain many elevating principles that need only to be modified by the doctrine of Christ to render them useful in preaching the Gospel. Far from ignoring such material, we should use it for our own purposes,

suet in his *Discours sur l'histoire universelle* and Schlegel in his *Philosophie der Geschichte* respected it. Cf. *supra*, Welldon, *St. Augustine De Civitate Dei*, p. l; J. P. Christopher, *St. Augustine: Founder of the Christian Philosophy of History*, p. 9.

[116] Migne, *Patr. lat.*, XXXIV, 15–122.

[117] *De doct. Chr.*; Migne, *Patr. lat.*, XXXIV, 56; *Nicene and Post-Nicene Fathers*, 1st ser., II, 549 f.

taking it from those who hold it unlawfully and restoring it to its rightful owners.

The fourth book of this treatise is a handbook of Christian rhetoric. The two characteristics most distinguishing it are its classical basis and its Christian spirit.[118] Here Augustine accepts the opinion of Cicero that the ends of eloquence are to instruct, to please, and to persuade. The rules of rhetoric are not to be acquired by adhering to hard and fast formulas, but by studying the best models. These models are especially the sacred writers and Christian authors, such as St. Cyprian and St. Ambrose. While the discourse should be pleasing so as to interest the audience and hold its attention, it must above all be clearly presented in order to be understood.[119] The object of the discourse is not to have the hearers declare that it was elegant, but to persuade them of the reasonableness of right living. It must bring home the truth to men so that they may understand it and practice it in their lives.[120]

In this work St. Augustine presents an analysis of ancient culture which, he is convinced, suffers from serious inherent defects. Up to this time all the Fathers, whether Greek or Latin, regarded ancient

[118] Sister Therese Sullivan, *S. Aureli Augustini Hipponiensis Episcopi De doctrina Christiana Liber Quartus* (Washington: The Catholic University of America, 1930), pp. 5 f.

[119] *De doct. Chr.*; Migne, *loc. cit.*, 99 f. *Nicene and Post-Nicene Fathers*, II, 582.

[120] Migne, *loc. cit.*, 116; *Nicene and Post-Nicene Fathers*, IV, 25, 55.

civilization as the only possible type of culture. They could not conceive of any other form any more than they could visualize a political organization other than the Roman Empire. Hence their attitude toward ancient civilization is critical rather than constructive. They criticize and correct but they do not look forward to building up a new culture. Augustine, on the other hand, realizes that ancient culture is decadent; there is little hope for it except in the way of preservation of its literary elements. A Christian scholar must, then, look forward to the future, to the reconstruction of culture on a thoroughly Christian basis.[121]

The *De doctrina Christiana* proposes a program of studies, not for elementary education, but for the secondary and higher levels of instruction; yet it does not attempt to project a plan for a Christian school in which the proposed program is to be carried out. We may rightly consider it a charter of Christian culture in the form of a manual announcing the doom of pagan culture. This educational treatise contemporary with that of Martianus Capella prepared the way for the future compilations of Cassiodorus and St. Isidore of Seville who labored to preserve for the Middle Ages what the past had bequeathed.[122]

[121] Henri-Irénée Marrou, *Saint Augustin et la fin de la culture antique* (Paris: E. De Boccard, 1938), VI, 354-56.
[122] Marrou, *op. cit.*, pp. 399-413.

Further pedagogical principles of Augustine are found in the *De catechizandis rudibus*, which has had a lasting influence on the history of catechizing, and its influence upon the catechisms of the Middle Ages is obvious. It is still highly regarded by the leaders in the field of religious instruction. The imprint of the principles of this classic in catechetical literature is seen in the many reforms of method and text-book which are regarded today as modern developments.[123]

In this work Augustine utilizes for religious instruction some of the best principles of sound pedagogy and psychology. It contains many valuable suggestions in regard to the teacher, the contents of instruction, and the methods most effective for the teaching of religion. Augustine urges the catechist not to confuse the candidate with too much material, but to insist on what is important and substantial and to explain it clearly and thoroughly; as far as possible, to give individual instruction; to adapt the instruction to the candidate's intelligence; to keep up interest, stimulate self-activity, and avoid tiring the memory; to attend to the bodily comfort of the candidate; to teach with a view to educating the candidate's heart as well as his mind; to have but one central theme, the love of God.[124]

[123] John T. McMahon, *Some Methods of Teaching Religion* (London: Burns, Oates and Washbourne, 1938), p. 1.
[124] Louis A. Rongione, "Saint Augustine's Principles on the Teaching of Religion as Presented in His De Catechizandis

The educational ideas which according to Augustine underlie the teaching process in general are exemplified in a practical way in the *De magistro*.[125] Here Augustine is seen in the role of teacher with pupil, in this case, Adeodatus his son. The keynote of the whole treatise is the attainment of truth and the means by which the mind of the pupil grasps it. Since what really does the teaching is the ability of the pupil's reasoning powers to see the truth or falsity of a proposition, the most marked principle of pedagogy employed by Augustine is pupil activity.[126] He points out that the pupil and not the teacher does the educating.[127] The chief function of teacher activity is to stimulate the pupil, both in study and recitation, to self-activity.

Regarding the use of language in the teaching and learning process, Augustine holds that words are nothing more than the expression of concepts. The realities signified by the words, not the words themselves, are the objects of knowledge.[128] This is the principle of objective teaching. As words can be interpreted only in the light of what a student knows, the interpretation of words comes through

Rudibus" (unpublished Master's dissertation, The Catholic University of America, 1940), p. 5. Cf. Christopher, *Augustinus De Catechizandis Rudibus*, pp. 4 f.

[125] Migne, *Patr. lat.*, XXXII, 1193–1220.
[126] *De magistro*, XIV, 45; Migne, *ibid.*, 1219 f.
[127] *Ibid.*, XII, 40; Migne, 1217.
[128] *Ibid.*, IX, 28; Migne, 1211.

previous knowledge which the mind has experienced.[129] Herein Augustine follows the doctrine of apperception. As there is nothing in the mind not first perceived by the senses, the importance of sense training in the learning process is evident. It is the function of the teacher, Augustine maintains, to bring into actuality by stimulation through the senses the potential capacities of learning which reside in the mind by nature.[130]

An effective means of stimulating thought and interest on the part of the pupil is the question method. Augustine emphasizes the use of this method in the first ten chapters of his treatise. He challenges the thinking of Adeodatus by clear and concise questions. Their searching character arouses the boy's interest and prompts his questions in return. Augustine is always careful that too much subject matter should not be presented to the pupil at any one time. The human mind learns step by step because of its incapacity to apprehend the whole truth in one comprehensive view.[131]

Another psychological principle of good teaching recognized by Augustine is the use of short and frequent reviews of knowledge, which aid the mind of the student in organizing what has been learned and serve as a foundation for further progress in the

[129] *Ibid.*, X, 33; Migne, 1214.
[130] *Ibid.*, XI, 36; Migne, 1215.
[131] *Ibid.*, XII, 40; Migne, 1217.

learning process. About halfway through the discussion he called on Adeodatus to review what had been treated,[132] and toward the end of the course he calls for a general review and asks him his opinions about the entire treatment.[133] A further aid in the educative process considered by Augustine is the solving of problems by the student. It is a teaching procedure through which solutions are obtained by the inductive and deductive method of thinking. Thereby knowledge that has been previously gained is practically applied and results in creative thinking.[134] Because the mind is developed by overcoming difficulties through serious and thoughtful thinking, Augustine suggests the creation of apparent objections, which the pupil must solve for himself, as a powerful means of developing mental growth. As an example of this he requires his pupil to answer the sophisms by which he had deceived him.[135]

Augustine is well aware that the instruction must be enlivened by little humorous digressions which serve to recreate the mind and prevent weariness. The jesting remarks made by a good teacher during the course of the discussion must not be regarded as futile.[136] Although Augustine conducted his lesson on a very informal level with the student at ease and

[132] *Ibid.*, VII, 19; Migne, 1206.
[133] *Ibid.*, XIV, 46; Migne, 1220.
[134] *Ibid.*, VIII, 23; Migne, 1208.
[135] *Ibid.*, VIII, 22; Migne, 1207 f.
[136] *Ibid.*, VIII, 21; Migne, 1207.

free to express himself, he does not minimize the authority of the teacher. He rightly regards the teacher as an extrinsic agent in the learning process, but he attributes to the teacher the knowledge of certain things which the student must accept on his authority.[137]

The *De magistro* of Thomas Aquinas is complementary to the *De magistro* of Augustine. Aquinas, in this instance, knew Augustine through the study of his work bearing the same title. In formulating the scholastic theory and philosophy of education, Aquinas bears witness that the *De magistro* of Augustine is a living document.[138]

The *De doctrina Christiana* and *De catechizandis rudibus* have been no less influential. The monastic schools, which, beginning with the sixth century, gradually supplanted the pagan schools of the grammarians and rhetoricians, were regulated in great part by the educational principles of these two works. Cassiodorus in his important manual of study for the interpretation of Holy Writ, *Institutiones divinarum et saecularium lectionum*, follows closely the educational doctrine of these two treatises. The *Etymologiae* of Isidore of Seville, which was a source book of information for centuries after its publica-

[137] *Ibid.*, XI, 37; Migne, 1215.
[138] John W. Tuohy, *The De Magistro of St. Augustine and the De Magistro of St. Thomas Aquinas Compared* (unpublished Master's dissertation, The Catholic University of America, 1937), p. 36.

tion in the seventh century, was based upon them. In England, Alcuin, under whom the cathedral school of York reached its highest development, used them as textbooks. His most distinguished pupil, Rhabanus Maurus, adapted them in the ninth century to his own purpose in composing the *De institutione clericorum* for the direction of the clergy and his students. In the Classical Renaissance, Petrarch, Erasmus, and Vives are leading humanist educators in debt to them.

Not only in the capacity of Christian teacher, but likewise as Christian philosopher, Augustine was an educator of remarkable influence. The debt that philosophy owes to him includes many original contributions to the definition of the Christian concept of God, of the human soul, and the destiny and duty of man.[189] He maintains, in particular, against the Neoplatonists, whom he regarded most highly among the ancient philosophers, the Christian theses that salvation is to be found in Christ alone, that divine worship is due only the triune God, that the soul with its body will rise again to eternal salvation or damnation, that the soul begins to exist at the same time as the body, that the world is perishable, and that only God and the spirits of angels and men are eternal. Against the dualism of the Manichaeans, he defends the monism of the good principle, explaining evil as a mere negation or privation. In opposition

[189] Turner, *History of Philosophy*, p. 234.

to Manichaeism and Gnosticism in general, he estab-
lishes the essential harmony between the Old and
New Testaments. Against the Donatists, he emphasizes the unity of the Church. In combating the
Pelagians, he asserts that divine grace is not condi-
tioned on human worthiness, but is a free gift of God
offered to some and not to others.[140]

The influence of Augustine on the philosophical
doctrines and method of Anselm is at once apparent.
Anselm looked to the writings of Augustine for confirmation of whatever he wrote. His ontological
argument is one of the many indications of the tendency of his mind to take the Augustinian view of
philosophical method. He has been fittingly styled
"the Augustine of the eleventh century." [141] Albertus Magnus and Thomas Aquinas, who followed
in the path of Anselm, likewise reveal the traditional Augustinian teaching that prevailed in the
schools. They held Augustine in honor and drew on
him when they chose.[142] Robert Grosseteste, the distinguished Franciscan teacher at Oxford, and his
brother in religion, Alexander of Hales, the equally
famous professor at Paris, although deep students of
Aristotle, were faithful disciples of Augustine. Bonaventure, who is indebted to Alexander of Hales for
much of his intellectual formation, recognized Au-

---

[140] Ueberweg, *History of Philosophy*, pp. 333 f.
[141] Turner, *op. cit.*, p. 278.
[142] Taylor, *The Medieval Mind*, 2nd ed., II, 435.

gustine as the inspiration of his theology, philosophy, and profound respect for tradition. The precursor of Bonaventure, Hugh of St. Victor, the twelfth century Scholastic, because of his familiarity with the works of Augustine, is sometimes spoken of as *Alter Augustinus*. He lived, wrote, and followed St. Augustine.[143]

The medieval Schoolmen looked upon Augustine as the master in theology, the great religious teacher. Never before or since was there given to the sacred sciences a thinker who, in writing about the action of God in his own soul, has somehow written the history of the hearts of all who read him.[144] The Middle Ages lived on his ideas. As Monsignor Duchesne has so well written of him:

He was the teacher of the whole of the Middle Age. In our own day still, after the decline inevitable to a supremacy of such long duration, he remains the great authority in theology. And above all it is through him that we get into touch with Christian antiquity. From some points of view he belongs to all ages. His soul and what a soul it is! has passed into his writings; in them he still lives.[145]

[143] Daniel C. O'Meara, *Educational Aspects of St. Augustine's Life and Works* (unpublished Master's dissertation, The Catholic University of America, 1921), p. 25.
[144] Hughes, *A History of the Church*, II, 27.
[145] Duchesne, *op. cit.*, III, vii.

CHAPTER V

THE PATRISTIC ATTITUDE
TOWARD PAGAN LEARNING

▰▰▰▰▰▰▰▰▰▰▰▰▰▰▰▰▰▰▰▰▰▰▰▰▰▰▰▰

THE attitude of the Fathers of the Church toward pagan learning may best be understood by our investigating the character of the state academies of the period and the opinions of the early Christian educators. The Church Fathers lived in direct contact with the pagan world and expressed themselves freely about the public schools of the Empire and the use of pagan literature in the Christian education of youth. Abundant evidence may be gathered from Christian writers to show a hostile tendency toward secular education.[1] This is not surprising if we take into account the persecution of the Church and the character of much of pagan literature. In the daily round of their life, Christians were witnesses of the idolatrous and sensual practices of the pagans. Coarseness and obscenity char-

[1] Cf. J. A. Lalanne, *Influence des pères de l'église sur l'education publique pendant les cinq premiers siècles de l'ère chrétienne* (Paris: Sagnier et Bray, 1850), p. 190.

acterized the circus, the theater, public exhibitions, and the institutions generally of the Graeco-Roman world.

Instruction in the ordinary Roman school was so closely bound up with religious ceremonies, and pagan literature required so much consideration of false gods and morals that the problem of reconciling secular education and the Christian faith was inevitable. Boissier, in describing this intimate connection between pagan learning and pagan religious life, indicates how difficult this problem was to solve.

Not only were all the ceremonies of the official faith—and more especially the festivals of Minerva, who was the patroness of masters and pupils—celebrated at regular intervals in the schools, but the children were taught reading out of books full of the old mythology. In the school the Christian child first became acquainted with the deities of Olympus. He was exposed to the danger of receiving ideas the very opposite of those which he had received at home. The fables he had learned in his home to detest were explained, commented upon, and admired every day by his master. Was it right to put him thus into two opposing schools of thought? What could be done that he might be educated like others, and yet not run the risk of losing his faith? [2]

What Augustine has told us of the schools of Carthage in his day proves that the public school continued to bear the stamp of its origin long after the

[2] Gaston Boissier, *La fin du paganisme* (Paris: Hachette et Cie, 1894), I, 200.

establishment of a nominal Christianity in the institutions of the Empire. The professors in the state
academies were the sophists by profession whose
chief concern was grammar and rhetoric. They were
interested not particularly in what was said but in
how it was said. Vile selections from the works of
the pagan authors were studied in which sexual life
with its morbid perversities held a prominent place.[3]
The teachers were not concerned about matters of
Christian faith or ethics; moral training was neither
given nor expected. In this regard there were noteworthy exceptions among the masters, but as a
general rule they were a pragmatical group that
emphasized the rules of learning to the neglect of
the eternal rules of salvation.[4] Breathing such an
atmosphere St. Gregory of Nazianzus declares that
it was as difficult for a youth to preserve his innocence as it would be for a river to preserve its fresh-
ness when flowing through the briny ocean.[5]

When under Constantine, early in the fourth century, Christianity became the religion of the Empire
and Christians were permitted to occupy the pro-
fessorial chairs, there were no textbooks in any of
the seven liberal arts except the treatises by pagan
authors. Declensions, conjugations, and the rules of
composition offered no danger to orthodoxy, but the

[3] *Confessions; Nicene and Post-Nicene Fathers*, I, 52 f.
[4] *Ibid.*, I, 53 f.
[5] Drane, *Christian Schools and Scholars*, p. 17.

illustrations dealing with phases of pagan thought and literature taken from infidel prose writers and poets raised perplexing problems for Church leaders with regard to education.[6] Converts who were teachers by profession were doubtful whether they should continue to teach.

In his treatise *On Idolatry*, Tertullian speaks of the professors in the pagan schools who are obliged "to preach the gods of the nations, to express their names, genealogies, honourable distinctions, all and singular; further to observe their solemnities and feast days because by means of them they are assured their salaries."[7] He felt that this perpetual handling and teaching of pagan mythology compromised the consciences of Christian teachers. He considered a Christian professor of Greek and Latin literature an idolater in disguise; yet he did not reject everything in classical culture, because he admits that "literature is the means of training for all life." Of him, Professor Rand has aptly remarked: "A professor of Greek and Latin, therefore, according to Tertullian, is a necessary evil; that is more courteous than what most people consider him to-day—an unnecessary evil."[8]

Tertullian is not an intransigent in treating the question of allowing Christians to share in pagan

[6] Laistner, *Thought and Letters in Western Europe*, p. 26.
[7] Tertullian, *De idololatria*, X; Migne, *Patr. lat.*, I, 674; *The Ante-Nicene Fathers*, III, 66 f.
[8] Rand, *Founders of the Middle Ages*, p. 41.

learning and literature. His sectarian rigor naturally enough prevented his approving Roman views and practices. Yet the fact that he is so severe in his condemnations of much that pagan culture contained, because he is so tender in his views of Christian training, is remarkable testimony to his sense of the all-importance of education and learning.[9] Being far too sensible of the advantages that an expurgated form of pagan literature would bring to the defense of Christianity, he was unwilling to reject those portions of it that could be used in the service of the true religion. His penetration led him to see that without secular studies divine studies could not be pursued effectively. Accordingly he advised giving Christian children the ordinary Roman education of the day. As a safeguard of their faith, he advocated that they should receive religious instruction at home and by this means be prepared to ignore the praises of the gods to which they listened. Tertullian's general feeling was that the knowledge of letters was so important as to justify some risks being incurred in its acquisition.

This point of view was shared by Christian parents who did not hesitate to send their sons to the public schools. Basil, Gregory of Nazianzus, Ambrose, and Augustine had attended the state academies and even taught in them. When Julian the Apostate attempted by law to close the public

[9] Hodgson, *Primitive Christian Education*, p. 199.

[163]

schools to Christians for the purpose of reducing the latter to an intellectual and practical helplessness, the protests of the Christians under the leadership of their bishops, notably Gregory of Nazianzus and Ambrose, show that they were unanimous in their regard for human learning.

It is certain that Christians in general did not approve the attendance of their children at the pagan schools. With the spread of monasticism, a specifically Christian education began. Christian parents now faced a momentous decision in regard to the public and monastic school for the education of their children. Chrysostom advises them to consider well the many dangers involved in sending their children to pagan schools. He knew from experience, as Augustine had known, that the paganism of the textbooks, of their companions, and of their teachers was a threefold danger for Christian youth. He tells us that in his knowledge of the character of the state schools the study of profane literature is not found united to the teaching of virtue. Despite the efforts of the Christian emperors, Constantine, Valentinian, Gratian, Honorius, and Theodosius, paganism struggled against Christianity, and nowhere did the pagan spirit manifest itself more than in the classroom. To the advantages that the public schools offered, Chrysostom owed the brilliant classical training which he brought with him into the Church. Indeed, he would have been among the last to underrate a liberal education and for that reason he is reluctant to determine for Christians a course of action that would place them at a disadvantage. However, after weighing the arguments for and against the public and the monastic school, he urged parents to send their children to the monasteries for their education. He writes:

If you have masters among you who can answer for the virtue of your children, I should be very far from advocating your sending them to the monastery; on the contrary, I should strongly insist on their remaining where they are. . . . But if no one can give such a guarantee, we ought not to send children to schools where they will learn vice before they learn science, and where, in acquiring learning of relatively small value, they will lose what is far more precious, their integrity of soul. . . . Are we then to give up literature? you will exclaim. I do not say that; but I do say that we must not kill souls.

When the foundations of a building are sapped we should seek rather for architects to reconstruct the whole edifice, than for artists to adorn the walls. . . . In fact, the choice lies between two alternatives; a liberal education which you may get by sending your children to the public schools, or the salvation of their souls which you secure by sending them to the monks. Which is to gain the day, science or the soul? If you can unite both advantages, do so by all means; but if not, choose the more precious.[10]

This passage is also important as showing that the monastery school very early educated children who

[10] Migne, *Patr. gr.*, XLVII, 367–71. Quoted from Drane, *op. cit.*, p. 20.

were destined for secular life as well as those who chose to become religious. It further implies that it was not possible for youth to receive a liberal education in the monastic schools. This may have been generally true in the time of Chrysostom, but in later centuries monastic learning was more fully developed. The fundamental aim of the monastery was to promote the glory of God. It was not primarily a school of arts and letters. Gradually the pursuit of learning was made an integral part of the pursuit of holiness, thus supplying a noble incentive toward intellectual studies. During the fifth and early sixth centuries many eminent churchmen, Cassian, Hilary of Arles, Faustus of Riez, Lupus of Troyes, Eucherius, Caesarius, were, at least in part, educated at monastic centers.[11]

The opinions of the eminent Fathers of the Church regarding the liberal arts and the place of pagan literature in a scheme of Christian education show that they recognized the propaedeutic value of the secular sciences in the lofty study and exposition of the Scriptures. With the spread of the Church, its contacts with the better educated classes of society became more intimate. There was need of a reasoned endeavor to convince rhetoricians, philosophers, and lawyers of the superior truths of the new faith. If the Christian apologists would be understood, they must use the language of the

[11] Laistner, *op. cit.*, p. 27.

schools. Although there was much in pagan literature and secular culture to avoid, Christianity was
obliged to draw on the thought and inspiration of
the past if letters and philosophy were to defend its
cause.

Lactantius in his *Divinae institutiones* gives a
sympathetic interpretation of the past. He was
splendidly equipped for writing the typical book of
his age. The old poets and philosophers were well
known to him. Not only is the influence of Lucretius, Horace, Ovid, Lucan, Persius, Juvenal, and
Vergil discernible in many of his ideas, but even less
known authors, like Ennius and Lucilius, are his
teachers. He finds in Plautus and Terence material
for moral instruction; Homer and Hesiod, though
sparingly quoted, furnish him with inspiration. The
classical author that exercises most influence on his
style and also on his whole manner of thinking is
Cicero.

There is no Christian writer from whom we can
get a truer notion of the attitude of the Church to
pagan learning than we get from Lactantius. The
standard set by him in this matter was in general respected by the Church. He asserted the principle
that, whereas pagan belief and pagan morals were
contrary to Christian faith, there was much in the
literature of the pagans that could be drawn on
freely for the furtherance of Christian teachings.[12]

[12] Rand, *op. cit.*, pp. 49–63.

The patristic program of studies did not make the ancient arts mere handmaids of the Church. Pagan literature was cultivated for its own sake. Jerome read Cicero "while he fasted, and devoured Plautus while he bewailed his sins." So as not to lose time on the road, he carried with him on his journey to Jerusalem a copy of Plato.

When the best in the literature of Greece and Rome had been adjusted to the Christian faith, the Fathers of the Church made less use of ancient resources and turned to the Sacred Scriptures as the source of those noble ideas which found expression in their moral and doctrinal treatises. In these writings the compelling motive of the Church Fathers was the salvation of souls. The Gospel of Christ directed all their efforts to eternal life. It drew all their mental energies to the work of understanding the faith and of interpreting it by means of the Scriptures. Their achievement was the establishment of ecclesiastical organization and the integration of Catholic doctrine.[13]

No one understood better than did Clement of Alexandria the usefulness of historical methods, of geometry, of astronomy, and especially of dialectics when used as a means in the interpretation of the truths of faith.[14] He neglected no branch of human learning in his efforts to defend the truth against

[13] Taylor, *The Medieval Mind*, p. 86.
[14] De Labriolle, *History and Literature of Christianity*, p. 24.

[168]

those who misunderstood it. He dwells on the fact that human arts come from God as really as the revelation of divine truth, asserting that the Greek philosophers borrowed from the Hebrew Scriptures. Origen in his school at Caesarea pressed upon Gregory Thaumaturgus the claims of philosophy, asserting that no one could be truly pious who did not philosophize.[15] He taught his pupils the various branches of learning common in the public schools. Through the instrumentality of secular literature he hoped to prepare them for a better understanding of the Christian faith.[16] Gregory of Nazianzus took the same attitude. He declared that secular literature has rendered a great service to the study of Christianity.

. . . And as we have compounded healthful drugs from certain of the reptiles; so from secular literature we have received principles of inquiry and speculation, while we have rejected their idolatry, terror, and pit of destruction. Nay, even these have aided us in our religion.[17]

Basil the Great maintained that the value of profane letters lies in the training which they give for a better understanding of the teachings of Scripture.

[15] Gregory Thaumaturgus, *Oration and Panegyric Addressed to Origen;* Migne, *loc. cit.,* 1017; *The Ante-Nicene Fathers,* VI, 27.

[16] Jerome, *Lives of Illustrious Men,* LIV; Migne, *Patr. lat.,* XXIII, 666.

[17] Gregory of. Nazianzus, *Panegyric on St. Basil;* Migne, *Patr. gr.* XXXVI, 507-10; *Nicene and Post-Nicene Fathers,* 2nd ser., VII, 398 f.

[169]

Youth receive from them a noble start in the formation of character, which they will complete later on by the study of the Bible. Not all that the pagan poets, orators, and historians wrote is contrary to a sound moral point of view. They provide many precepts and examples suited to ennobling the mind of a young man. Basil insists on a proper selection in dealing with secular literature.

We ourselves, too, if we are wise, having appropriated from this literature what is suitable to us and akin to the truth, will pass over the remainder. And just as in plucking the blooms from a rose-bed we avoid the thorns, so also in garnering from such writings whatever is useful, let us guard ourselves against what is harmful. At the very outset, therefore, we should examine each of the branches of knowledge and adapt it to our end, according to the Doric proverb, "bringing the stone to the line." [18]

Jerome in his turn defended the practice of adjusting the best in ancient literature and ancient thought to the Christian faith, despite the fact that he had resolved to give up reading pagan books. He was so devoted to the classics that he tells us he was rebuked in a dream because of his excessive fondness for profane authors.

[18] Quoted from Roy J. Deferrari and Martin R. P. McGuire, Basil The Great's *To Young Men, On How They Might Derive Profit from Pagan Literature.* Translated in the Loeb Classical Library (London: William Heinemann, Ltd., 1934), pp. 391–93.

After many nights spent in vigil, after floods of tears called from my inmost heart, after the recollection of my past sins, I would once more take up Plautus. And when at times I returned to my right mind, and began to read the prophets, their style seemed rude and repellent. I failed to see the light with my blinded eyes; but I attributed the fault not to them, but to the sun. . . . About the middle of Lent a deep-seated fever fell upon my weakened body, and while it destroyed my rest completely—the story seems hardly credible—it so wasted my unhappy form that scarcely anything was left on me but skin and bone. Meantime preparations for my funeral went on; my body grew gradually colder, as the warmth of life lingered only in my throbbing breast. Suddenly I was caught up in the spirit and dragged before the judgment seat of the Judge; and here the light was so bright, and those who stood around were so radiant, that I cast myself upon the ground and did not dare to look up. Asked who and what I was, I replied: "I am a Christian." But He who presided said: "Thou liest, thou art a follower of Cicero and not of Christ. For where thy treasure is, there will thy heart be also. . . ." Accordingly I made oath and called upon His name, saying: "Lord, if ever again I possess worldly books, or if ever again I read such, I have denied Thee." [19]

Jerome did not renounce the classics completely. When he was accused by Rufinus of relapsing into Ciceronianism and thereby breaking his solemn promise given in the dream of Cicero, he retorted that it was only a dream, and a vow made in a dream does not bind us. Throughout his letters numerous

[19] *Epist.* 22; Migne, *Patr. lat.*, XXII, 416 f.; *Nicene and Post-Nicene Fathers*, 2nd ser., VI, 35 f.

citations from pagan authors are to be found. In his seventieth letter he points out that the tradition of quoting from secular literature goes back beyond St. Paul, right to Moses and the prophets. Christians can find erudition and philosophy in all the books of the profane authors with the possible exception of Epicurus. His strictures regarding the study of pagan authors were never absolute.[20] By an allegorical simile he justifies his position toward them by recalling the despoiling of the Egyptians without pollution from the spoils. He also vindicates his views by advocating the use of secular literature in the interests of the faith in much the same way as the command given by God in Deuteronomy ordered the captive woman to be purified before she was taken to wife.

Augustine, like Jerome, also employs an allegorical simile in which he illustrates the use that may be made of secular learning. As the Jewish people in the flight from Egypt took from their enemies vessels of gold and silver and appropriated them to their own use by the command of God, so the Christian must take from pagan literature its gold and silver, liberal instruction, and some excellent principles of morality, and adapt them to Christian use.

For, as the Egyptians had not only the idols and heavy burdens which the people of Israel hated and fled from, but also vessels and ornaments of gold and silver, and gar-

[20] Laistner, *op. cit.*, p. 29.

ments, which the same people when going out of Egypt, appropriated to themselves, in their ignorance, providing them with things which they themselves were not making a good use of; in the same way all branches of heathen learning have not only false and superstitious fancies and heavy burdens of necessary toil, which every one of us, when going out under the leadership of Christ from the fellowship of the heathen, ought to abhor and avoid; but they contain also liberal instruction which is better adapted to the use of the truth, and some most excellent precepts of morality; and some truths in regard even to the worship of one God are found among them. . . . These, therefore, the Christian, when he separates himself in spirit from the miserable fellowship of these men, ought to take away from them and devote to their proper use in preaching the Gospel.[21]

It is true that in his *De doctrina Christiana*, Augustine is seen not only as the man of letters but also as the Christian rigorist.[22] He asserts that the study of the liberal arts should cease as early as possible. There is little need for profane literature because the treasures of the Holy Scriptures are vastly superior to the riches which the Christian takes from secular learning to the study of these sacred writings.[23] Yet the chapters that conclude this treatise are modeled on Cicero's *De oratore*, thus indicating

[21] *De doct. Chr.*; Migne, *Patr. lat.*, XXXIV, 63; *Nicene and Post-Nicene Fathers*, 1st ser., II, 554.

[22] De Labriolle, *op. cit.*, p. 27.

[23] *De doct. Chr.*; Migne, *Patr. lat.*, XXXIV, 63; *Nicene and Post-Nicene Fathers*, 1st ser., II, 555.

that Augustine respects truth wherever it may be found.[24]

In the record thus handed down it is evident that there were periods of revolt against pagan culture. In fact, anathemas were more than once pronounced against it. In 398 the Fourth Council of Carthage formally forbade even the bishops to read pagan books. There was, however, no complete break with the civilization of the Graeco-Roman world. Christianity had adopted the ancient culture as part of its own. At the dawn of the Middle Ages, the pagan authors had a fixed place in Christian education. The views of the medieval Schoolmen concerning secular learning were formed not only through their own reading of classical literature and by the opinions of contemporaries, but by what was determined from the early Christian centuries under the signature of a Basil the Great, a Lactantius, an Ambrose, a Jerome, and an Augustine.[25]

[24] Laistner, *op. cit.*, p. 33.
[25] Rand, *op. cit.*, pp. 280 f.

CHAPTER VI

SUMMARY

▄▄▄▄▄▄▄▄▄▄▄▄▄▄▄▄▄▄▄▄▄▄▄▄▄▄▄▄▄▄▄▄▄▄▄▄▄▄▄

IT was in the Roman Empire, externally progressive but internally degenerate, that Jesus Christ was born. With His Incarnation a new era began in the history of education. Christ Himself declared that He was the Savior of all men, that His gospel should be preached throughout the world. To ensure the permanence of His teaching, He founded the visible Church and commanded His disciples to go and teach all nations. From the very beginning the Church felt deeply the obligation imposed by this teaching office and became a true educational institution.

/ The great educational work of the Church was initiated by the apostles under the guidance of the Holy Ghost. It was continued and was advanced with remarkable success by the Fathers of the Church, who gradually combined the work of the Christian schools with the liberal arts of Graeco-Roman culture. Among them are to be found eminent scholars and teachers. In the East, St. Justin

Martyr was the first to attempt a philosophy of Christian thought; Clement of Alexandria distinguished himself as the headmaster of the catechetical school in that city and was highly regarded for his extraordinary learning; Origen, the first great scholar among the Christian Fathers, conducted a famous school at Caesarea; St. Athanasius, the champion of the divinity of Christ, was a subtle dialectician; St. Cyril of Jerusalem formulated a series of catechetical instructions, *Catecheses*, which are of especial importance in the history of catechetics; the three Cappadocians, St. Basil the Great, St. Gregory of Nyssa, and St. Gregory of Nazianzus, brought to the service of the Church all the culture and learning of their time; St. John Chrysostom, once a celebrated lawyer, became the patriarch of Constantinople and merited the title "Great Teacher of the Earth"; Dionysius the Pseudo-Areopagite was the author of a number of theological works whose influence in Western theological science in subsequent centuries was unequaled by any other work of the Greek Patristic; later, in the eighth century, St. John of Damascus gathered the scattered teaching of earlier theologians into a great compendium called the *Fountain of Wisdom*, which to this day is the standard work of theology in the orthodox East.

It would be an error to conclude that the educational work of the Fathers of the Church proceeded wholly along theological lines. In the catechetical

schools the major courses of study were instruction
in the Scriptures and in theology; but, in an effort to
counteract skepticism, paganism, and the views of
opposing sects, these institutions offered a literary
training and instruction in all the sciences then
studied and in all the systems of philosophy except
the Epicurean because it was so sensual. Origen con-
firms this point of view when counseling his pupil,
Gregory Thaumaturgus, in his school at Caesarea.

But I am anxious that you should devote all the strength
of your natural good parts to Christianity for your end;
and in order to do this, I wish to ask you to extract from
the philosophy of the Greeks what may serve as a course
of study or a preparation for Christianity, and from geometry and astronomy what will serve to explain the sacred
Scriptures, so that all that the sons of the philosophers
are wont to say about geometry and music, grammar,
rhetoric and astronomy, as fellow-helpers to philosophy,
we may say about philosophy itself in relation to Christianity.[1]

The Western Church Fathers are the disciples of
the Fathers of the East. From their Greek masters
they learned lessons in an original way, improving
what they learned and finding new truth for themselves. Although not opposed to speculation and
dialectic, they are preoccupied with practical and
moral problems.

The Fathers of the West are distinguished writers

[1] Quoted from Hodgson, *Primitive Christian Education*,
p. 204.

[177]

and professional educators. Tertullian inaugurated
Latin Christian literature. Despite his unsound reputation from the point of view of orthodoxy, he exercised a marked influence as the first Latin interpreter
of Christian thought in the West. The qualities of
St. Cyprian as a writer were recognized throughout
the Christian world and gained for his works universal respect. Lactantius was regarded as a model of
Ciceronian elegance. His philosophical treatise in
defense of Christianity is the first attempt by a Western writer to give a systematic exposition of Christian theology. Although it contains errors which
show the author's lack of accurate interpretation of
the Scriptures, numerous copies of this manuscript
were made down to the Renaissance.

The fourth and fifth centuries are the ages of the
great doctors in the West. St. Hilary, St. Ambrose,
St. Jerome, and St. Augustine are the four great
Christian leaders in this era. By reason of their ecclesiastical prominence and their wide acquaintance
with sacred and profane knowledge, they were most
influential in molding medieval thought.

The well-deserved reputation of St. Hilary as a
teacher merited for him the distinction of being
designated Doctor of the Universal Church. So
vigorously did St. Ambrose defend the Church's
teaching and ecclesiastical discipline that he was
rightly regarded in succeeding ages as the great
Father of medieval Christianity. The whole life of

SUMMARY

St. Jerome was devoted to study. His scholarship and humanism made his influence profound and enduring in the centuries that came after him. St. Augustine, the last and greatest of the doctors of the Church in the golden age of the Latin Fathers, was the recognized theological authority from the beginning of the fifth century. He became the foremost teacher of the Middle Ages.

Augustine, Jerome, and their distinguished predecessors directed all intellectual interests toward the building up of Christian doctrine and ecclesiastical supremacy. The great concern of the Fathers was the understanding and defense of the faith. Every intellectual inquiry was subordinate to this need. In their efforts to define and maintain the faith they investigated all provinces of secular learning with a view to drawing from them whatever supported the teachings of the Christian religion and discarding what was irrelevant and ephemeral.[2]

The achievement of the Fathers of the Church was Catholic Christianity, consisting of ecclesiastical organization and the consistent organism of doctrine.[3] Through their energy and intellectual power, Church and doctrine were constructed and made ready for transmission to the Middle Ages.

The Church Fathers were the practical educators in the patristic period, which includes mainly the

[2] Taylor, *The Medieval Mind*, 4th ed., 1930, I, 62.
[3] *Ibid.*, p. 86.

first five centuries of the Christian era. Many of them were bishops ultimately responsible for the moral and religious education of youth; others were teachers in the catechetical schools, profoundly interested in methods of teaching.

The voluminous writings of these men, particularly the works of Augustine, inspired the educational achievements of the medieval Schoolmen. The Christian heritage bequeathed in the patristic literature of the Eastern and Western Church was the foundation upon which the Scholastics built a well-defined system of schools.

BIBLIOGRAPHY

■▪■

The following selection of books comprises a few works of general and particular interest accessible in English.

General

Ayer, Jr., J. C. *Source Book of Church History for the First Six Centuries*. New York: Charles Scribner's Sons, 1913. 707 pp.

Bardenhewer, Otto. *Patrology*. Translated from the second German edition by Thomas J. Shahan. St. Louis: B. Herder Company, 1908. 680 pp.

Bardy, Abbé. *The Christian Latin Literature of the First Six Centuries*. Paris, 1928. Translated by Mother Mary Reginald, O.P. London: Sands and Company, 1930. 222 pp.

Battifol, Pierre. *Primitive Catholicism*. Translated from the fifth French edition by Henri L. Brianceau. New York: Longmans, Green and Company, 1911. 424 pp.

Belloc, Hilaire. *Europe and the Faith*. New York: The Paulist Press, 1920. Chapters 1-6.

Bigg, Charles. *The Christian Platonists of Alexandria*. New York: The Macmillan Company, 1886. 304 pp.

Bright, William. *The Age of the Fathers*. London: Longmans, Green and Company, 1903. 2 vols.

Bury, John B. *History of the Later Roman Empire*. London: Macmillan and Company, 1923. 2 vols.

Campbell, James M. *The Greek Fathers*. New York: Longmans, Green and Company, 1929. 167 pp.

Cubberley, Ellwood P. *Readings in the History of Education*. Boston: Houghton Mifflin Company, 1920. Chapter 4.

D'Arcy, M. C., *et al*. *The Life of the Church*. New York: The Dial Press, 1932. 27–159 pp.

Davidson, Thomas. *A History of Education*. New York: Charles Scribner's Sons, 1901. Chapter 5.

Dawson, Christopher. *The Making of Europe*. London: Sheed and Ward, 1932. 317 pp.

———. *Progress and Religion*. New York: Sheed and Ward, 1938. 254 pp.

Dill, Samuel. *Roman Society from Nero to Marcus Aurelius*. London: Macmillan and Company, 1920. 639 pp.

Drane, Augusta T. *Christian Schools and Scholars*. London: Burns, Oates and Washbourne, 1924. Chapter 1.

Duchesne, Louis. *Histoire Ancienne de l'Eglise*. Paris, 1906–10. 3 vols. English translation, London: John Murray, 1909–24.

Duff, J. Wight. *The Writers of Rome*. London: Oxford University Press, 1923. 109 pp.

Eby and Arrowood. *The History and Philosophy of Education Ancient and Medieval*. New York: Prentice-Hall, 1940. Chapters 10–14.

Fisher, George P. *History of Christian Doctrine*. New York: Charles Scribner's Sons, 1909. 583 pp.

Fortescue, Adrian. *The Greek Fathers*. St. Louis: B. Herder Company, 1908. 255 pp.

Fowler, Harold N. *A History of Roman Literature*. New York: The Macmillan Company, 1928. Chapters 18–20.

BIBLIOGRAPHY

Fuerst, A. N. *The Systematic Teaching of Religion*. New York: Benziger Brothers, 1939. Chapter 3.

Gibbon, Edward. *The Decline and Fall of the Roman Empire*. John B. Bury, editor. London: Methuen and Company, 1896–1938. 7 vols.

Glover, Terrot R. *Life and Letters in the Fourth Century*. Cambridge: Cambridge University Press, 1901. 398 pp.

————. *Conflict of Religions in the Early Roman Empire*. 5th ed. London: Methuen and Company, 1920. 359 pp.

Goodier, A. *The Public Life of Our Lord Jesus Christ*. London: Burns, Oates and Washbourne, 1930. 2 vols.

Graves, Frank P. *History of Education*. Vol. I, *Before the Middle Ages*. New York: The Macmillan Company, 1909. Chapters 13–14.

Gwynn, Aubrey. *Roman Education from Cicero to Quintilian*. Oxford: Clarendon Press, 1926. 260 pp.

Harnack, A. *The Mission and Expansion of Christianity in the First Three Centuries*. Leipzig: J. C. Hinrichs, 1902. Translated into English by James Moffatt. London: Williams and Norgate, 1904–5. 2 vols. Second enlarged and revised edition. New York: G. P. Putnam's Sons, 1908.

Hodgson, Geraldine. *Primitive Christian Education*. Edinburgh: T. and T. Clark, 1906. 287 pp.

Hughes, Philip. *A History of the Church*. London: Sheed and Ward, 1935. Vol. I, x–395 pp. Vol. II, chapters 1–2.

Kane, W. *An Essay toward a History of Education*. Chicago: Loyola University Press, 1935. Chapters 5–6.

Kidd, B. J. *History of the Church to A.D. 461*. Oxford: The Clarendon Press, 1922. 3 vols.

Labriolle, Pierre de. *History and Literature of Christian-*

ity. Translated by Herbert Wilson. New York: Alfred A. Knopf, 1925. 555 pp.

Laistner, M. L. W. *Thought and Letters in Western Europe*. New York: The Dial Press, 1931. 354 pp.

Laurie, S. S. *Historical Survey of Pre-Christian Education*. New York: Longmans, Green, and Co., 1900. 301–411 pp.

Leigh-Bennett, E. *Handbook of the Early Christian Fathers*. London: Williams and Norgate, 1920. 340 pp.

McCormick, Patrick J. *History of Education*. Washington: The Catholic Education Press, 1915. Chapters 7–9.

Magevney, Eugene. *Christian Education in the First Centuries*. New York: The Cathedral Library Association, 1907. 61 pp.

Marique, Pierre J. *History of Christian Education*. New York: Fordham University Press, 1924. Vol. I, chapters 1–2.

Merrill, Elmer T. *Essays in Early Christian History*. London: Macmillan and Company, 1924. Chapter 10.

Monroe, Paul. *Text-Book in the History of Education*. New York: The Macmillan Company, 1921. Chapters 4–5.

Moore, Clifford H. *The Religious Thought of the Greeks*. Cambridge: Harvard University Press, 1925. 2nd. ed. 385 pp.

Moore, Ernest C. *The Story of Instruction: The Beginnings*. New York: The Macmillan Company, 1936. Chapter 6.

———. *The Story of Instruction: The Church, and Renaissance, and the Reformations*. New York: The Macmillan Company, 1938. Chapters 1–3.

Newman, John Henry. *Historical Sketches*. London:

Longmans, Green and Company, 1896. Vol. II, 487 pp.

Ramsey, W. M. *The Church in the Roman Empire before 170*. New York: G. P. Putnam Sons, 1893.

Rand, Edward K. *The Founders of the Middle Ages*. Cambridge: Harvard University Press, 1928. 365 pp.

Sandys, John E. *A History of Classical Scholarship*. New York: The Macmillan Company. Vol. I, 3rd ed., 1921. 701 pp.

Shahan, Thomas J. *The Beginnings of Christianity*. New York: Benziger Brothers, 1903. 445 pp.

Sihler, Ernest G. *From Augustus to Augustine*. Cambridge: University Press, 1923. 335 pp.

Swete, Henry B. *Patristic Study*. New York: Longmans, Green and Company, 1902. 194 pp.

Taylor, Henry O. *The Classical Heritage of the Middle Ages*. New York: Columbia University Press, 1901. 400 pp.

———. *The Medieval Mind*. New York: Macmillan and Company, 1930. 4th ed. 2 vols.

Turner, William. *History of Philosophy*. Boston: Ginn and Company, 1903. Section B. 30–236 pp.

Ueberweg, Friedrich. *History of Philosophy*. Translated from the 4th German edition by George S. Morris. New York: Charles Scribner's Sons, 1892. Vol. I. 487 pp.

Westcott, B. F. *The Religious Thought of the West*. New York: Macmillan and Company, 1891. 142–252 pp.

Wilkins, A. S. *Roman Education*. Cambridge: University Press, 1914. 100 pp.

Willmann, Otto. *Didaktik als Bildungslehre nach ihren Beziehungen zur Socialforschung und zur Geschichte der Bildung*. Braunschweig: F. Vieweg und Sohn,

1894–95. 2 vols. Translated under the title *Science of Education* by Felix M. Kirsch, O.M. Cap., from the fifth German edition. Beatty, Pa.: Archabbey Press, 1930, 2nd edition. Vol. I, 170–95.

Particular

(Note. In this list the following abbreviations are used:
AN Fathers = The Ante-Nicene Fathers;
N and PN Fathers = A Select Library of the Nicene and Post-Nicene Fathers.
Both are published by Charles Scribner's Sons, New York.)

Ambrose, St. *De officiis*. N and PN Fathers, 2nd ser., Vol. X.

Athanasius, St. *Vita S. Antonii; Orationes IV contra Arianos*. N and PN Fathers, 2nd ser., Vol. IV.

Augustine, St. *Confessiones; De Civitate Dei; De doctrina Christiana*. N and PN Fathers, Vols. I and II.

———. *De catechizandis rudibus*. Translated by Joseph P. Christopher. Washington: The Catholic University of America, 1926. 15–121 pp.

———. *De Magistro*. Translated under the title of *The Philosophy of Teaching* by Francis E. Tourscher. Villanova: Villanova College, 1924. 99 pp.

Basil, St. *De Spiritu Sancto*. N and PN Fathers, 2nd ser., Vol. VIII.

———. *Address to Young Men on the Right Use of Greek Literature*. Translated in *Essays on the Study and Use of Poetry by Plutarch and Basil the Great* by Frederick M. Padelford. New York: Henry Holt and Company, 1902; translated in the Loeb Classical

BIBLIOGRAPHY

Library by Roy J. Deferrari and Martin R. McGuire. London: William Heinemann, 1934.

Bruce, A. B. *The Parabolic Teaching of Christ.* 3rd ed., 1908. New York: A. C. Armstrong and Sons. 515 pp.

Chase, F. H. *Chrysostom, a Study in the History of Biblical Interpretation.* Cambridge: Deighton, Bell and Company, 1887. 204 pp.

Chrysostom, St. *De sacerdotio; Homiliae XXI de statuis ad populum Antiochenum.* N and PN Fathers, 1st ser., Vol. IX.

————. *Golden Book of St. Chrysostom, Concerning the Education of Children.* Translated by John Evelyn in *The Miscellaneous Writings of John Evelyn* by William Upcott. London: Henry Colburn, 1825.

Clement of Alexandria. *Protrepticus; Paedagogus; Stromata.* AN Fathers, Vol. II.

Cyprian, St. *Epistolae; De Catholicae Ecclesiae unitate.* AN Fathers, Vol. V.

Cyril, St. *Catecheses.* N and PN Fathers, 2nd ser., Vol. VII.

Dudden, Frederick H. *The Life and Times of St. Ambrose.* Oxford: Clarendon Press, 1935. 2 vols.

Gregory of Nazianzus, St. *In Defense of His Flight; Theological Orations; The Panegyric on St. Basil.* N and PN Fathers, 2nd ser., Vol. VIII.

————. *Orationes invectivae contra Julianum Imperatorem.* Translated under the title of *Julian the Emperor* by C. W. King. London: George Bell and Sons, 1888.

Gregory Thaumaturgus, St. *Oration and Panegyric Addressed to Origen.* AN Fathers, Vol. VI.

Hilary of Poitiers, St. *De Trinitate.* N and PN Fathers, 2nd ser., Vol. IX.

[187]

Jerome, St. *De viris illustribus.* N and PN Fathers, 2nd ser., Vol. III.

——. *Epist.* 107, 128. N and PN Fathers, 2nd ser., Vol. VI. Also translated in the Loeb Classical Library by F. A. Wright (London: William Heineman) under the title *Select Letters of St. Jerome.* Epist. 107 is translated with the exception of a few paragraphs in *Barnard's American Journal of Education,* V, 593–98.

John of Damascus, St. *De fide orthodoxa.* N and PN Fathers, 2nd ser., Vol. IX.

Justin, St. *Apologies; Dialogue with Trypho.* AN Fathers, Vol. I.

Lactantius. *Divinae institutiones; Epitome divinarum institutionum.* AN Fathers, Vol. VII.

Origen. *De principiis; Contra Celsum.* AN Fathers, Vol. IV.

Rolt, C. E. *Dionysius the Areopagite, On the Divine Names and the Mystical Theology.* London: Society for Promoting Christian Knowledge, 1920. 223 pp.

Tertullian. *Apologeticum; De idolatria; De spectaculis; Ad nationes; Adversus Marcionem.* AN Fathers, Vol. III.

——. *De cultu feminarum; De virginibus velandis; De monagamia.* AN Fathers, Vol. IV.

INDEX

INDEX

Augustine, St. (*continued*)
De magistro, 142, 152-55: relation to *De magistro* of St. Thomas, 155
De musica, 143
De Trinitate, 140 f.
Retractationes, 141

Bacon, Francis, 147 note
Barbarossa, 98
Basil the Great, St., 43, 58, 67-71, 174, 176: *Address to Young Men*, 71 f.; *De Spiritu Sancto*, 70; patriarch of Oriental monasticism, 69 f.; work against Eunomius, 71
Benedict, St., 62
Bernard, St., 134
Boissier, 160
Bonaventure, St., 89, 93, 157 f.
Burgundio, Joannes, 98

Caesar, 15
Caesarius, 166
Cambrensis, Geraldus, 147
Cappadocians, the three, 66 f., 90
Carthage, Fourth Council of, 174
Cassian, 133, 166
Cassiodorus, 62, 89, 111, 150
Cato the Elder: collection of sayings, 7; *De liberis educandis*, 7; opposition to Greek influences, 6 f.; "Rem tene, verba sequentur," 7; Roman curriculum, 13
Catullus, 15
Charlemagne, 147
Charles the Bald, 93
Christ; *see* Jesus Christ
Christianity, reason for spread of, 18-20
Chrysostom, St., 80-90, 176
Adversus oppugnatores vitae monasticae, 88

Chrysostom, St. (*continued*)
advice to parents, 165
corporal punishment, 85
De liberis educandis, 84
De sacerdotio, 78, 81, 83
development of Christian character, 88
"Doctor Eucharistiae," 83
doctrine of imitation, 88
education of girls, 87
educational philosophy, 84
exegetical methods, 83
"Great Teacher of the Earth," 80
home training, 88
Homilies on the Statues, 81
influence of, 88
parental example, 85
principle of emulation, 88
sex instruction, 87, 89
theory of learning, 85
training for citizenship, 88
use of scriptural stories, 86
vocational guidance, 88
Cicero, 167: *De oratore*, 15
Civilization, early Western, 21
Clement of Alexandria, 43, 46-51, 176
catechetical school, 47, 51: curriculum of, 50
Christianity and Hellenism, 47
Exhortation to the Greeks, 48
Human arts and divine revelation, 169
influence on theological science, 51
Introduction to Christianity, 48
moral education, 49
The Pedagogue, 48 f.
physical education, 49
sources of references, 51
Stromata, 48, 50
Comana, 82
Combesis, Francis, 84
Constantine, 110, 161, 164

[190]

INDEX

Constantinople, Second Council of, 64
Cosmas, 95
Crispus, 110
Cucusus, 82
Cyprian, St., 16, 32, 106-9, 178
  bishop of Carthage, 107
  De Catholicae Ecclesiae unitate, 108
  influence of, 108 f.
  martyrdom of, 107
  regard for Tertullian, 106
  writings of, 108
Cyril of Alexandria, St., 90 note
Cyril of Jerusalem, St.
  Catecheses, 58, 64 f., 176
  class of catechumens, 66
  homoousios, 63
  method of teaching, 66
  mystagogical instruction, 65
  Procatechesis, 64

Damasus, St., (pope), 124, 127
Dante, 147
Darboy, 94
Decius, 107
Demetrius, 52
Denys of Paris, 93
Dianius, 68
Diocletian, 110
Dionysius the Pseudo-Areopagite, 91-93, 176: influence of, 93 f.; writings of, 91
Donatus, 123

Education, Christian: contrast with pagan, 23; during first two centuries, 32
Education, Roman, 8, 12, 14; *see also* Schools
  borrowings from the Greek, 15
  contrast with Greek, 1-3
  decline of interest in schools, 17
  early, 3

Education, Roman *(continued)*
  Greek influence, 5-7
  literary training, 4
  physical training, 4
  wandering lecturers, 17
Einhart, 147
Emmelia, 68
Ennius, 167
Epicureans, 38
Epiphanius, 95
Erasmus, 89, 134, 156
Erigena, John Scotus, 93
Eucherius, 166
Eudoxia, 82
Eunomius, 71
Eusebius of Caesarea, 59 note
Eustathius, 68
Eustochium, 125
Evelyn, John, 84

Fathers of the Church: attitude toward pagan learning, 159; definition of term, 43
Fathers of the East, 43 f.: many educated in public schools, 43; some as teachers in public schools, 43
Fathers of the Golden Age, 58
Fathers of the West, 99
Faustus of Riez, 166
Filelfo, 134
Flavian, 81

Galerius, 110
Gaudentius, 129
Gennadius, 127
Gnosticism, 135, 157: St. Irenaeus' *Adversus haereses*, 54 note
Graeco-Roman period, instruction during, 9
Gratian, 118, 164
Grosseteste, Robert, 93, 157
Gregory of Nazianzus, St., 67, 76-79, 164, 176
  Apology for His Flight, 77

INDEX